The Holy Bible — Revelation

F&SF Ministry For JESUS

MARCH WAS WHEN JESUS WAS BORN AND <u>NOT</u> CHRISTMAS
(Not Santa Claus Day)

People born in March should be interested in reading this Book.

By: Apostle Frederick E. Franklin

authorHOUSE®

AuthorHouse™
1663 Liberty Drive
Bloomington, IN 47403
www.authorhouse.com
Phone: 1-800-839-8640

Published by AuthorHouse 5/9/2013

ISBN: 978-1-4817-2975-8 (sc)
ISBN: 978-1-4817-2974-1 (e)

Library of Congress Control Number: 2013905011

Any people depicted in stock imagery provided by Thinkstock are
models, and such images are being used for illustrative purposes only.
Certain stock imagery © Thinkstock.

This book is printed on acid-free paper.

Because of the dynamic nature of the Internet, any web
addresses or links contained in this book may have changed
since publication and may no longer be valid.

The views expressed in this work are solely those of the author
and do not necessarily reflect the views of the publisher, and
the publisher hereby disclaims any responsibility for them.

TABLE OF CONTENTS

INTRODUCTION

This book is our (34th) thirty-fourth book which we have written. Shortly after we finished writing our (33rd) thirty-third book, "A Man Named Bush Prepares The Way For The Anti- Christ," God said that we should write this book. We finished writing the (33rd) thirty-third book on December 11, 2001. At the time when God said we should write a (34th) thirty-fourth book, we had no idea what we would be writing on. In fact, we only learned, God told us on Friday, afternoon, November 14, 2003.

This is a life changing book. As our cover implies, we will show you that JESUS' birthday is not Christmas. We will show that the Christmas extravaganza was before JESUS was born. We will show you that it was, even, in the Old Testament of the Holy Bible. You will be shocked/astonished several to many times when you read this book. We will show, by scripture, the actual month JESUS was born. We will even provide the day of the month for JESUS' birth. We believe we will even show the day that JESUS was born. The greatest skeptic, if you believe the Holy Bible, will agree with us. Much, much, more will you learn. Yes, and like most of our (33rd) thirty-third previous books, we will give you revelation from God about the end times. Even related to Christmas. Even related to JESUS' birth; THE MARCH BIRTHDAY.

MARCH WAS WHEN JESUS WAS BORN AND NOT CHRISTMAS

Christmas is the most cherished day among people on earth. There is no day to compare with it. It is loved by nearly all the earth. It is loved by sinners, so-called Christians and Christians/Saints. Atheist, those who say there is no God, love this day. Other sinners, (barbarians, infidels, heathens, so-called Christians, Christian hypocrites, idol god worshippers, etc.) love and cherish the Christmas event.

Sinners, as we will show should love Christmas. A sinner is one who has not been born again. One who professes to be a Christian and one who is actually born again should not love Christmas. One who is born again/saved is defined in scriptures of the Holy Bible.

John Ch, 3, Vs. 3-5
"Jesus answered and said unto him, Verily, verily, I say unto thee, Except a man be born again, he cannot see the kingdom of God. Nicodemus saith unto him, How can a man be born when he is old? Can he enter the second time into his mother's womb, and be born? Jesus answered, "Verily, verily,

I say unto thee, Except a man be born of the water and of the Spirit, he cannot enter into the Kingdom God"

The so-called Christians say that they celebrate Christmas because it is JESUS' birthday. Ironically, even hypocritically, some that say that "JESUS is the reason for the season", implying, that if it was not for it being JESUS' birthday, then they would not celebrate Christmas. They realize and understand that others realize, that the Christmas extravaganza is such a contradiction to the Holy Bible and is full of lies. The god of Christmas, Santa Claus, is said to be omniscience, know all things. The lie is said that he knows when you are good or bad. The so-called Christian and Christian/Saints know that God of the Holy Bible is the only one who is omniscience. They know that God hates lies. Yet, Christmas is full of lies that, even, they understand to be lies.

Isaiah Ch. 40, V. 28
"Hast thou not known? Hast though not heard, that the everlasting God, the LORD, the creator of the ends of the earth, fainted not, neither is weary? There is no searching of his understanding."

Isaiah Ch. 46, V. 9
"...for I am God, and there is none else; I am God, and there is none like me."

<u>Isaiah Ch. 44, Vs. 24 &25</u>
"Thus saith the LORD, thy redeemer, and he that formed thee from the womb, I am the Lord that maketh all things; that stretcheth forth the heavens alone; that spreadeth abroad the earth by myself; that frustrateth the tokens of the liars, and maketh diviners mad; that turneth wise men backward, and maketh their knowledge foolish..."

<u>Psalm 139, Vs. 1-4</u>
"O Lord, thou hast searched me, and known me. Thou knowest my downsitting and mine uprising, thou understandeth my thought afar off. Thou compassest my path and my lying down, and art aquatinted with all my ways. For there is not a word in my tongue, but. Lo, O LORD, thou knowest it altogether."

<u>Psalm 86, V. 8</u>
"Among the gods there is none like unto thee..."

The so-called Christians and Christians/Saints know, then, to say that Santa Claus is omniscience, is to say that God is a liar which is blasphemy. It is said about Santa Claus, that he knows when you are good or bad. The so-called Christians and Christians/Saints know that God hates lies. Yet, they tell their children these lies. Yet, they help support these lies.

Proverbs Ch. 6, Vs. 16 & 17
"...the LORD hate: Yea, ...an abomination unto him: ...a lying tongue..."

Psalm 101, V. 7
"He that worketh deceit shall not dwell within my house: he that telleth lies shall not tarry in my sight."

Christmas is an extravaganza of lies. Not only what we have already mentioned, but there are more lies associated with Christmas that the so-called Christians and Christians/ Saints know to be lies. Other of these lies are:

1. Santa Claus riding on a sled;
2. Santa Claus sled being pulled by reindeers;
3. A reindeer's nose glows;
4. Santa Claus gives the children gifts;
5. Santa Claus delivers all the children their gifts in one night;
6. Santa Claus comes down a chimney;
7. Santa Claus puts gifts in a stocking;
8. A big fat man having a long white beard with a red and white furry suit is Santa Claus and only he gives the children their gifts;
9. Santa Claus lives at the north pole;
10. Santa Claus makes the Christmas gifts along with his helpers called elves;

11. The weather forecasters on the Christmas night news' cast can spot Santa Claus flying through the air;

12. A reindeer can fly;

13. Etc.

With all these being lies, sinners probably look at so-called Christians and Christians/Saints as being great hypocrites. Surely a Holy God would not have pleasure in being associated with a lie.

Revelation Ch. 21, V. 8
"But the fearful, and unbelieving, and the abominable, and murders, and whoremongers, and sorcerers, and <u>idolaters, and all liars,</u> shall have their part in the lake which burneth with fire and brimstone: which is the second death."

Revelation Ch. 22, Vs. 14 & 15
"Blessed are they that do his commandments, that they may have right to the tree of life, and may enter in through the gates into the city. For without are dogs, and sorcerers, and whoremongers, and murderers, and <u>idolaters</u>, and <u>whosoever loveth and maketh a lie.</u>"

Revelation Ch. 21, Vs. 10 & 27
"...and shewed me that great city, the holy Jerusalem, descending out of heaven from God... And there shall in no wise enter into it any thing that

defileth, neither whatsoever worketh abomination, or <u>maketh a lie</u>: but they which are written in the Lamb's book of life."

Some non so-called Christians and some non Christians/Saints, must be astonded at so-called Christians and Christians/ Saints. So-called Christians and Christians/Saints, say that they believe that the Holy Bible is the word of God. The non so-called Christians and non-Christians/Saints are faithful to obey their gods and their top god Satan.

The Holy Bible tells us to train our children up in the way of the teachings of the word of God. No wonder that the world's, including some Christian's/Saints' children, <u>are liars</u>. The <u>first lies</u> learned by children are from their parents associated with Christmas.

<u>Proverbs Ch. 22, V. 6</u>
"Train up a child in the way he should go: and when he is old, he will not depart from it."

Even if all we have said thus far was not so, Christmas participation should not be so by the so-called Christians and Christians/Saints. If they indeed love God as they say, they would not participate in activities associated with Christmas.

I John Ch. 2, V. 15

"Love not the world, neither the things that are in the world. If any man love the world, the love of the father is not in him."

So-called Christians and Christians/Saints, know that Christmas is the most beloved time of all the world.

You might say, as a so-called Christian or Christian/Saint, that it is a good thing for so much attention to be focused on JESUS' birthday. Well, now we must show that Christmas is not JESUS' birthday.

The Christmas event, which was not so called by that name, has been around for thousands of years. It was around thousands of years before JESUS was born. The extravaganza is pagan worship of idol gods. There is clear evidence of such worship of this idolatry in the Holy Bible. The extravaganza has its origins and history with the heathens worshipping their idol gods associated with the heavens.

In ancient Egypt the god was Ra. This same like worship of the false gods of the heavens continued throughout history, including during the Roman Empire days. This worship of the Romans was the worship of the idol god Zeus. Connected with this worship was the worship of Arthemis and Dianna.

Have you wondered why the Catholic Church worships Mary? The Catholic Church put more emphasis on Mary than JESUS. This Mary worship has its roots in ancient idolatry also. The goddess Arthemis and goddess Dianna are the sources for the worship of Mary. The idol god Zeus was the heathens' second top god during the time of the Roman Empire, second only to Satan. As the lie says, Zeus had a daughter named Arthemis. Arthemis, as the lie says, was the goddess of virginity, the goddess of childbirth, even, mother of gods. Dianna was the Roman equivalent to Arthemis. So can you now see why the Catholic Church worships Mary? Mary the virgin. Mary who was pregnant who never had sex with a man. Mary the mother of God/JESUS.

Apostle John, one of JESUS twelve (12) disciples, was the last Apostle to die. He died after being exiled to an unpopulated island called Isle of Patmos. He was sent there to prevent him from preaching that JESUS was God. After Apostle John died, there was a struggle for power to see who then who then would be over God's Church. There was a man in the City of Rome who won this struggle for power. So the ones to follow him would then always rule. Not as God wanted, but as the desires of power greedy men they ruled. The ruler in Rome was eventually called the Pope.

In about 325 A.D., the then Pope came in a agreement with the Emperor of Rome named Constantine. They agreed to tell the lie, to the so-called Christian world, that the birth of JESUS was the same as the day of the worship of their Roman idol god. This day, as the lie says, is when their goddess birth their god, one of their idol gods. To appease the so-called Christians and to make it more acceptable, they agreed to call that day Christ mass. Christ mass was eventually called Christmas. During this 325 A.D. abominable conference, there were, also other abominable lies agreed on. Some other of these abominations are:

1. To say that JESUS was raised from the dead on Easter which is worship of the Spring goddess;
2. To not baptize in the name of JESUS as Apostle John and the other Apostles had said and done, but rather to baptize, saying, I baptize you in the name of the Father, the Son, and of the Holy Ghost;
3. Etc.

Refer to our Book "JESUS Was Not Crucified When As Has Been Taught".

We mentioned earlier that there is Biblical evidence of Christmas events before JESUS was born. We now show you this evidence. In the Holy Bible we can see the use of so-called Christmas trees being used in the heathen's idolatry and Israel's disobedience in worship of idol gods. The Bible refers to the equivalent of the Christmas trees as groves. Groves are small trees.

After the children of Israel were delivered out of Egypt which served the idol god Ra; God instructed/ commanded the children of Israel not to participate in the Christmas equivalent idolatry of the heathen nation.

Exodus Ch. 34, Vs. 11-13
"Observe thou that which I command thee this day; behold, I drive out before thee the Amorite, and the Canaanite, and the Hittite, and the Perizzite, and Hivite, and Jebusite. Take heed to thyself, lest thou make a covenant with the inhabitants of the land whither thou goest, lest it be for a snare in the midst of thee: But ye shall destroy their altars, break their images, and cut down their groves ..."

Deuteronomy Ch. 12, V. 3
"And ye shall overthrow their altars, and break their pillars, and burn their groves ..."

Deuteronomy Ch. 16, V. 21
"Thou shall not plant thee a grove of any tree near unto the altar of the LORD thy God ..."

Judges Ch. 3, V. 7
"And the children of Israel did evil in the sight of the LORD, and forgat the LORD their God, and served Baalim and the groves."

Judges Ch. 6, V. 25
"... the LORD said unto him ... throw down the altar of Baal ... and cut down the grove that is by it ..."

Baal was an idol god.

I Kings Ch. 16, V. 33
"And Ahab made a grove; and Ahab did more to provoke the LORD God of Israel to anger more than all the Kings of Israel that were before him."

I Kings Ch. 18, V. 19
"...the prophets of Baal four hundred and fifty, and the prophets of the groves four hundred, which eat at Jezebel's table."

II Kings Ch. 17, V. 16
"And they left all the commandments of the LORD their God, and made them molten images, even two calves, and make a grove, and worshipped all the host of heaven, and served Baal."

II Kings Ch. 21, Vs. 1-3
"Manasseh was twelve years old when he began to reign ...And he did that which was evil in the sight of the LORD, after the abominations of heathens ...

and he reared up altars for Baal, and made a <u>grove,</u> as did Ahab King of Israel ..."

<u>II Kings Ch. 22, Vs. 1&2; Ch. 23, V. 4</u>
"Josiah ... did that which was right in the sight of LORD ... the king commanded ... to bring fourth out of the temple of the LORD ... all the vessels that were made for Baal, and for the <u>grove,</u> and for all the host of heaven: and he burned them ..."

<u>II Kings Ch. 23, Vs. 15</u>
"... he brake down, and burned the high places and stamped it small to powder, and burned the <u>grove.</u>"

<u>II Chronicles Ch. 34, V. 3</u>
"... he began to purge Judah and Jerusalem from the high places, and the <u>groves,</u> and the carved images, and the molten images."

<u>Micah Ch. 5, V. 14</u>
"And I will pluck up thy <u>groves</u>, out of the midst of thee: so will I destroy the cities."

You might say, so what, yes I believe that God hated the groves. Yes, I believe that God hated the groves. Yes, I believe that the use of groves is idolatry. Yes, groves are an abomination to God. This, you might say, however, does not show that groves are equivalent to Christmas trees. Well consider these scriptures also.

Jeremiah Ch. 10, Vs. 1-5

"Hear ye the word of which the LORD speaketh unto you, O house of Israel: thus saith the LORD, Learn not the way of the heathen, and be not dismayed at them. For the customs of people are vain: <u>for one cutteth a tree out of the forest, the work of the hands of the workman, with the ax. They deck it with silver and gold; They fasten it with nails and with hammers, that it move not; they are upright as the palm tree...</u>"

Well, these days you might not cut the tree out of the forest with an ax. You probably will use a chain saw. Well, these days you might not decorate the Christmas tree with gold and silver. You probably will use the colors of silver and gold, and also red, blue etc. Maybe you use those things call Christmas lights. Well, something has not changed. They made a stand with a hammer and nails to keep the tree stable. In these days we do the same. This tree of Jeremiah is a tree of the groves. Now consider these scriptures.

II Kings Ch. 23, Vs. 5-7

"And he put down the idolatrous priest,...them also that burned incense unto Baal, to the sun, and to the moon, and to the planets, and to all the host of heaven. And he brought out the <u>grove</u> from the house of the LORD...and he burn it, and stamped to small powder...And he brake down the houses of the sodomites, that were by the house of the LORD, where the women wove hangings for the <u>grove</u>."

Well in these days, the women do not have to weave decoration to hang on The Christmas tree. You go and buy those silvery things, called garland, to put on the Christmas tree.

[Note This. This is an insert to the Book before it went in to publication. In the fall of the Year we call 2012, God gave me a great revelation. Look again at the above Scriptures, II Kings Ch. 23, Vs. 5-7, God said "And he brake down the houses of the sodomites, that were by the house of the LORD, where the women wove hangings for the grove". God told me that Christmas was and is the Sodomites Religion. There are many in idolatry on this earth, at the present time, such as, those that are in the Buddha Religion, Hindu Religion, Muslim Religion, etc., but only the Sodomites are in the idolatry of Santa Claus/Christmas. This is their religion brought down through history.]

Another component of the Christmas extravaganza

that has roots in idolatry is for Santa Claus to hold the little children in his arms. This has its roots in baby sacrifice. It was the custom of the heathens to place their babies in the arms of their big fat idol god for a sacrifice. It is our understanding that the Moabites also, where some of these heathens that did this abominable custom. When God's angels got Lot and his daughters out of Sodom, God destroyed Sodom. Moab was influence by Sodom through Lot's daughters. In fact Moab was the son of Lot. The Moabites, thereby, were influenced by the culture of Sodom. Moab was both a son and grandson of Lot; This also was a custom of Canaanites.

Psalm 106, Vs. 34 -38

"They did not destroy the nations, concerning whom the LORD commanded them: But were mingled among the heathens, and learn their works. And they served their idols: Which were a snare unto them. Yea, they sacrificed their sons and their daughters, whom they sacrificed unto the idols of Canaan: and the land was polluted with their blood."

The Canaanites are now named Palestinians. The so-called Christians and the Christians/Saints might say, so, what is the Big Deal; we, you might say, are not having our children killed? We then ask you this, as a so-called Christian or Christian/Saint, would you, symbolically or otherwise, lay your baby or young child in the arms of a Buddha stature as part of any celebration? Would you? Well, that is what you are doing when you lay your baby or young child in the arms of Santa Claus.

We will now show you that the scriptures of the Holy Bible tell us clearly that JESUS was not born on Christmas Day. It is amazing how Santa, we mean Satan, has been able to blind us to keep us from the truth of when JESUS was born. The Holy Bible says that JESUS was born on a day when an angel appeared unto some shepherds while their sheep was in the field eating grass.

<u>Luke Ch. 2, Vs. 7-11</u>
"And she brought forth her firstborn son, and wrapped him in a swaddling clothes, and laid him in a manger; because there was no room in the inn. And there were in the country shepherds abiding in the field, keeping watch over their flock by night. And lo, the angel of the Lord came upon them and the glory of the Lord shone round about them: and they were sore afraid. And the angel said unto them, fear not: for, behold, I bring you good tidings of great joy, which shall be to all people. For unto you is born this day in the city of David a Savior, which is Christ the Lord."

Note, the shepherds were in the field with the sheep eating grass, even green grass. There is no grass in the fields in the winter for the sheep to eat over in the Holy Land. The sheep are fenced in and fed hay in the winter. It, therefore, was not winter when JESUS was born. It was not December. It was not December 25th when JESUS was born. It was not Christmas when JESUS was born.

You, might say, that this is not totally convincing to me. Well, we will now give you proof positive, that JESUS was not born on Christmas. We saw this scriptural proof after many years of being blinded by Santa, we mean Satan. Even after we finally had come to the truth that JESUS was not born in Christmas, we did not see this very obvious scriptural proof. God finally, however, remove the blindfold from our eyes that we might see. This is how it happened. One day, a Friday, God had us to get our Bible. We just picked it up and laid it open on our study desk at home. God then spoke to us to search the scriptures for proof that JESUS was not born on Christmas. We had read the scriptures over and over again for this proof, but the best proof we could discover is what we have, thus far, written. So, when God spoke to us about searching the scriptures, we began to think of what else could we study. Then it came to our mind to look again at the scriptures related to when Herod killed the children of the area called Ramah. This is the town where children, two years or less, were killed in Herod's attempt to kill JESUS when he was born. We could not remember exactly where the scriptures were located in the Bible. We then picked up our concordance that was on our study desk to find where the scriptures were located. We found that it was located in Jeremiah Chapter 31, Verse 15. We then went to get the Bible to find that scripture. Incredibly, astonishingly, as we looked at the open Bible on the desk, the first thing we saw right before our eyes was Jeremiah Chapter 31, Verse 15. We knew at this point that God was getting ready to show us something about when JESUS was born. We then read this scripture, but we did not see anything that we had not seen before.

Jeremiah Ch. 31, V. 15
"Thus saith the LORD; a voice was heard in Ramah, lamentation, and bitter weeping, Rachel weeping for her children refused to be comforted for her children, because they were not."

We did not receive any kind of revelation from God by reading this scripture, so we just figured that God must have had this happen to encourage us to look further. Then God spoke to us to read Luke Chapter 1. We had read this Chapter many times before, so we wondered what we could find now. As we began to read, we saw nothing new. We kept reading Luke Chapter 1, again and again. We just never saw why God told us to read this. One time we thought we had discovered something new, but the study of the scriptures proved this to be wrong. This, however, lead us to what God was trying to show us by reading Luke Chapter 1. There it was right before our eyes, and we just kept reading over it. Satan had blinded us. It took no revelation from God to understand. But, we had not seen it. Custom and tradition thinking had blinded us. Even a carnal mined person could see it. We felt so very stupid for not seeing it before now. There it was. The truth that God wanted us to see was in Luke Chapter 1, Verse 5.

<u>Luke Chapter 1, Verse 5.</u>
"There was in the days of Herod, the King of Judaea, a certain priest named Zacharias, of the course of Abia: and his wife was the daughter of Aaron, and her name was Elizabeth."

You might say, I still do not get it. First, let us give a little background then we will show the significance of Luke Chapter 1, Verse 5.

Zacharias was a priest that at this time was old. His wife was Elizabeth. She, also, was old. In their youthful years, they had prayed for God to give them a son, but Elizabeth could never get pregnant. One day, in his old age, Zacharias was performing his duties as a priest, and an angel appeared unto him. The angel told him that Elizabeth would finally get pregnant and bare him a son. The angel said that his name would be called John. This is the John that was called John the baptist. Amazingly, Zacharias did not believe the angel. This was the angel Gabriel. Well, to make a short summary of it, when Zacharias left the Temple where and when he had finish his duties as a priest, he went home. In process of performing his manly husband duties, Elizabeth got pregnant.

Luke Chapter 1, Vs. 23& 24

"And it came to pass, that as soon as the days of his ministration were accomplished, he departed to his own house. And after those days his wife Elizabeth conceived …"

Elizabeth had a young woman as a cousin called Mary. When Elizabeth was six months pregnant, her cousin Mary conceived. This is the Mary whom was the mother of JESUS of Nazareth; the mother of the Son of God. This was the conception of JESUS CHRIST, the Son of God.

Luke Chapter 1, Vs. 26-28 & 30-31

"And in the <u>sixth month</u> the angel Gabriel was sent from God unto a city of Galilee, name Nazareth, to a virgin exposed to a man named Joseph, of the house of David; <u>and the virgin name was Mary.</u> And the angel came in unto her, and said, hail thou that art highly favored, the Lord is with thee: blessed art thou among women. And the angel said unto her, Fear not, Mary: for thou shalt conceive in thy womb, <u>and bring forth a son,</u> and shalt call his name <u>JESUS."</u>

Luke Chapter 1, Vs. 34-36

"Then said Mary unto the angel, How shall this be, seeing I know not a man? And the angel answered and said unto her, The <u>Holy Ghost</u> shall come upon thee, and the power of the Highest shall overshadow thee: therefore also that holy thing which shall be born of thee shall be called the Son of God. And, behold, thy cousin Elizabeth, she hath also conceived a son in her old age: and this is the <u>sixth month</u> with her, who was barren."

So, we clearly see that JESUS was six months younger than John the Baptist.

Now, let us get back to the significance of Luke Chapter 1, verse 5. Again let us look at this verse.

<u>Luke Chapter 1, V. 5</u>

"There was in the days of Herod, the King of Judaea, a certain priest named Zacharias, of the course of Abia: and his wife was the daughter of Aaron, and her name was Elizabeth."

To understand the significance of the above scripture in determining when JESUS was born, you must understand the <u>courses.</u> When David was King of Israel he wanted to build God a temple. God, however, would not allow David to do so. God said because David had blood on his hands, he would not allow David to do so. We suppose that God looked at David's hands, as defiled hands that would pollute the temple. David had, during his adulterous affair with Bethsheba, had her husband <u>Uriah</u> killed. Even though, at this time David had repented, yet he was not allowed to build the Temple of God. God told David he would not allow him to build His Temple, but he would allow his son Solomon to build the Temple. Solomon was King after David. God, however, did allow David to do things in preparing for the Temple, for when it would be eventually built. Among these things, God allowed David to lay out a plan of how and when the priests would perform duties in the Temple. This time of performing duties for priest was called a course. A course lasted a complete month. This duty allocation by David was from month to month continually. A certain priest for a month year round. The first course was in the first month, the second was in the second month, the third course in the third month, and so on.

I Chronicles Ch. 23, Vs.1, 2 &6
"So when David was old and full of days, he made Solomon King over Israel. And he gathered together all the princes of Israel, with the priest and Levites. And David divided them into courses ..."

I Chronicles Ch. 23, V.13
"The sons of Amram; Aaron and Moses: and Aaron was separated, that he should sanctify the most holy thing, he and his sons forever, to burn incense before the LORD, to minister unto him, and to bless in his name for ever ..."

I Chronicles Ch. 27, Vs.1 &2
"... month by month throughout all the months of the year, of every course ... Over the first course for the first month ..."

I Chronicles Ch. 24, Vs.1, 5 &7- 10
"Now these are the divisions of the sons of Aaron ... Thus were they divided by lot, one sort with another; for the governors of the things of God ... Now the first lot came forth to Jehoiarib, the second to Jedaiah, The third to Harim, the fourth to

<u>Seorim</u>, <u>the fifth</u> to Malchujah, <u>the sixth</u> to <u>Mijamin</u>, <u>the seventh</u> to <u>Hakkoz</u>, <u>the eight</u> to <u>Abijah</u> ..."

A lot was a chosen allocation assigned to each particular course/month. The first lot with the first course, the first month. The second lot with the second course, the second month. The third lot with the third course, the third month and so on. After the twelfth lot with the twelfth course, the thirteen lot starts at the first course, the first month. The fourteenth lot with the second course, the second month. The fifteenth lot with the third course, the third month and so on. Ending with the twenty-fourth lot with the twelfth course, the twelfth month.

"Abijah" in the above scriptures, I Chronicles Ch. 24, Vs. 1,5&7-10, is also spelled Abia; these are the two different spellings of the same word in the Old Testament and the New Testament of the Holy Bible respectively. Abijah/Abia did service as a priest in the eighth course which is done in the eighth month. Let us now go back to Luke Chapter 1.

<u>Luke Chapter 1, V. 5</u>
"There was in the days of Herod, the King of Judaea, a certain priest named Zacharias, of the <u>course of Abia</u>: and his wife was the daughter of Aaron, and her name was Elizabeth."

This means <u>Elizabeth</u> became pregnant in the ninth month. This means Mary conceived the Son of God JESUS, six months after the <u>ninth month</u>. She, <u>Mary</u>, <u>conceived</u> in the third month. This means that JESUS, the Son of God, was <u>born in twelfth month.</u>

You might say, hold on now, it said in I Chronicles Chapter 24, Verse 1, that the scriptures were talking about the Sons of Aaron. But, you might say, Luke Chapter 1, Verse 5, mentioned Elizabeth was of the daughter of Aaron. It did not say, you might say, that Zacharias was the son of Aaron. Yes, you are right. But, both Elizabeth and Zacharias is from the scriptures of I Chronicles Chapter 23, Verse 13 and Luke Chapter 1, Verse 8 & 9. Both Elizabeth and Zacharias were of the lineage of Aaron.

<u>I Chronicles Ch. 23, V. 13</u>
"The sons of Amram; Aaron and Moses: and Aaron was separated, that he should sanctify the most holy thing, he and his sons forever, to <u>burn incense</u> ..."

<u>Luke Chapter 1, Vs. 8& 9</u>
"And it came to pass, that a while he executed the priest's offices before God in order of his courses, According to the custom of the priest's office, his lot was burn incense ..."

The sons of Aaron were priest and only the sons of Aaron could burn incense.

You might say, ok, ok, ok I believe you! So, you might say, I believe you that JESUS was born in the twelfth month. But, this just proves that JESUS was born in December. No! No! No! The twelfth month of the Holy Bible is not the twelfth month of our calendar. The twelfth month in the Holy Bible is the month of Adar. The month of Adar is normally the time of our month of March. JESUS was therefore, born in Adar/March.

The Jewish calendar months as God said them to be, starts in the month of Abib. Abib starts in March or April. Listed below are the Jewish Calendar months as stated in the Holy Bible.

The First Month
(Is called Abib or Nisan)

Deuteronomy Ch. 16 V. 1
"Observe the month of Abib, and keep the Passover unto the LORD thy God: for in the month of Abib the LORD thy God brought thee forth out of Egypt by night."

Exodus Ch. 12, Vs. 1, 2 & 12
"And the LORD spoke unto Moses and Aaron in the land of Egypt, saying, this month shall be unto

you the beginning of the months: <u>it shall be first month of the year to you</u>. For I will pass through the land of Egypt this night, and I will smite all the first born in the land of Egypt, both man and beast, and against all gods of Egypt I will execute judgment: I am the LORD.

<u>Ester Ch. 3 V. 7</u>
"In <u>the first month</u>, that is, the month of Nisan, in the twelfth year of King Ahasuerus, they cast Pur, that is, the lot, before Haman from day to day ..."

<u>The Second Month</u>
(Is called Zif)

<u>I Kings Ch. 6 V. 1</u>
"And it came to pass in the four hundred and eightieth year after the children of Israel had come out of the land of Egypt, in the fourth year of Solomon's reign over Israel, in the month of <u>Zif, which is the second month</u> that he began to build the house of the LORD."

<u>The Third Month</u>
(Is called Sivan)

<u>Ester Ch. 8 V. 9</u>
"Then the King's scribed called at that time in <u>the third month, that is, the month of Sivan</u>, on the

three and twentieth day thereof; and it was written according to all that Mordecai commanded ..."

The Fourth Month
(There is no Biblical name for the Fourth Month. The Fourth Month has been called Tammuz.)

Jeremiah Ch. 39 V. 2
"And the Eleventh year of Zedekiah, in the fourth month, the ninth day of the month, the city was broken up."

The Fifth Month
(There is no Biblical name for the Fifth Month. The Fifth Month has been called Ab.)

Numbers Ch. 33 V. 38
"And Aaron the priest went up into the mount Hor at the commandment of the LORD, and died there, after the fortieths year after the children of Israel had come out of the land of Egypt, in the first day of the fifth month.

The Sixth Month
(Is called Elul)

Nehemiah Ch. 6 V. 15
"So the wall was finished in the twenty and fifth day of the month of Elul, in the fifty and two days.

The Seventh Month
(Is called Ethanim or Tisri)

I Kings Ch. 8, V. 2
"And all the men of Israel assembled themselves unto King Solomon at the feast in the month Ethanim, which is seventh month.

The Eighth Month
(Is called Bul)

I Kings Ch. 6, V. 38
"And the eleventh year, in the month Bul, which is the eighth month, was the house finished throughout all the parts thereof, and according to all the fashion of it. So was he seven years in building it."

The Ninth Month
(There is no Biblical name for the Ninth Month. The Ninth Month has been called Chisleu.)

Ezra Ch. 10, V. 9
"Then all the men of Judah and Benjamin gathered themselves unto Jerusalem within three days. It was the ninth month, on the twentieth day of the month; and all the people sat in the streets of the house of God, trembling because of this matter, and for the great rain."

The Tenth Month
(Is called Tebeth)

Ester Ch. 2, V. 16
"So Ester was taken unto King Ahasuerus into his house royal in the <u>tenth month</u>, which is the <u>month Tebeth</u>, in the seventh year of his reign."

The Eleventh Month
(Is called Sebat)

Zachariah Ch. 1, V. 7
"Upon the four and twentieth day of the eleventh month, which is the month Sebat, in the second year of Darius, came the word of the LORD unto Zachariah, the son of Berechiah, the son of Iddo the prophet ..."

The Twelfth Month
(Is called <u>Adar</u>)

Ester Ch. 3, V. 7
"...They cast Pur, that is, lot, before Haman from day to day, and from month to month, to the <u>twelfth month</u>, that is the <u>month Adar</u>."

Listed below are the Jewish Calendar's months and the months as we have known them:

1. <u>Abib or Nisan</u>, the first month (late March or April)

2. <u>Zif</u>, the second month (late April or May)
3. <u>Sivan</u>, the third month (late May or June)
4. <u>Tammuz</u>, the fourth month (late June or July)
5. <u>Ab</u>, the fifth month (late July or August)
6. <u>Elul</u>, the sixth month (late August or September)
7. <u>Ethanim or Tisri</u>, the seventh month (late September or October)
8. <u>Bul</u>, the eighth month (late October or November)
9. <u>Chisleu</u>, the ninth month (late November or December)
10. <u>Tebeth</u>, the tenth month (late December or January)
11. <u>Sabet</u>, the eleventh month (late January or February)
12. <u>Adar</u>, the twelfth month (late February or March)

As the scriptures have shown and will show, <u>JESUS</u> was <u>conceived</u> in the third month, the <u>month of Sivan</u>, the month of June. Nine months later JESUS was born in the month of <u>Adar</u>, the month of March. JESUS, therefore, was not born in December, the month of Chisleu. JESUS, therefore, was <u>not </u>born on Christmas.

You might ask, why are you saying JESUS was born in March rather February ? We say this because of the Passover as we will show you later. We will show you this, but for right now let us point out this. The above truth and facts about when JESUS was born, leaves no more excuses, at all for so-called Christians and Christians/Saints to celebrate Christmas. Some have said, you might say, that you do not see anything wrong with praising and worshipping JESUS, whether it be on Christmas or any other time. After all, you might say, people sing songs related to JESUS on Christmas. People, you might say, read the scriptures related with JESUS on Christmas. You might say, it is the only time when people will go to church. During Christmas, you might say, is when people show love more than any other time by giving gifts to others.

Well, it is plenty wrong with your stubborn justification to, yet participate in idolatrous Christmas activities. JESUS of Nazareth the Son of God, being God Almighty's body here on earth, does not desire a coinciding praise or worship with a little idol god. God is a great King. The King of kings. The God of gods. The Lord of lords. The Creator of all, natural and spiritual, that was and that is. God does not share glory with any. He is the one and only majestic and supreme God. He is God that has all dominion and control.

Matthew Ch. 15, Vs. 1,3& 9
"...JESUS...said unto them, why do ye also transgress the commandment of God by your tradition? But in vain they worship me, teaching for doctrines the commandments of men."

Psalm 47, V. 2
"For the LORD most high is terrible, he is a great King over the earth."

Psalm 95, V. 3
For the LORD is a great God, and a great King above all gods."

Malachi Ch. 1, V. 14
"... for I am a great King, saith the LORD of hosts, and my name is dreadful among the heathen."

Deuteronomy Ch. 10, V. 17
"For the LORD God is God of gods, and the LORD of lords, a great God, a mighty, a terrible, which regardeth not persons, nor taketh reward..."

Revelation Ch. 19, V. 16
"And he hath on his vesture and on his thigh a name written, KING of KINGS, and LORD of LORDS."

As we indicated earlier, God has nothing to do with lies. You cannot mix the lies of Christmas with the praise and worship of God.

John Ch. 4, V. 24
"God is a spirit: and they that worship him must worship him in spirit and in truth."

God is not interested in and desirous of everyone worshipping him. The great numbers during Christmas, that goes to church and that sing songs mentioning JESUS, do not impress God.

Proverbs Ch. 15, V. 8
"the sacrifice of the wicked is an abomination unto the LORD: but the prayer of the upright is his delight."

Proverbs Ch. 28, V. 9
"He that turneth his ear away from hearing the law, even his prayer shall be abomination."

Proverbs Ch. 21, V. 1
"The King's heart is in the hand of the LORD, as the rivers of water: he turneth it whithersoever he will."

Psalm 75, Vs. 6& 7
"For promotion cometh neither from the east, nor the west, nor from south, but God judge: he putteth down one, and setteth up another."

Revelation Ch. 4, V. 11
"Thou art worthy O Lord, to receive glory and honor and power: for thou has created all things, and for thou pleasure they are and were created."

How could you think such a God as this, would share praise with an abominable idol god? In language you might understand, how could you think such a God as this, would share the spotlight with the idolatrous Christmas' Santa Claus? You would not, dare, share, even the birthday celebration of a leader of a country with an unknown person. Not, even, a person of some substantial worldly significance. Not even, a person of a lower status than that certain leader.

As a so-called Christian and Christian/Saint, you should not have any involvement whatsoever, with Christmas and its associated activities. We first came to the understanding that we should not celebrate Christmas back in December, 1989. This is when we were living in Montgomery, Alabama. God sent a woman evangelist and prophetess all the way from Palo Alto, California, to tell us that it is wrong to celebrate Christmas. So we decided that the Christmas coming up, that we would not put up a Christmas tree, nor give or receive Christmas gifts. We decided that on Christmas, we would go out of town to Mobile, Alabama and visit family members and relatives. On our visit with family and relatives that Christmas, they tried to give us gifts, but we said we could not receive them. We told them we could not give or receive Christmas gifts any longer, because we had found out that it was wrong to do so and Christmas was not when JESUS was born. They were shocked that we would say this. They did not accept what we had said. They tried to force us to take gifts and we just continued to refuse. They felt so very sorry for us. They even thought that we must have, undoubtedly, loss our minds. They finally stop trying to get us to receive gifts. Then we all started to open gifts they had received. Afterward, we all sat down to eat a big good looking, good tasting, Christmas dinner. On our way back to Montgomery from Mobile, God began to rebuke us. He told us we that had been partakers of the Christmas idolatry. He said that we should not have opened those Christmas gifts. He said we should not have eaten that Christmas dinner. He said we should have not have eaten that Christmas candy and nuts. He said we should, not, have, even, been in their midst during Christmas related celebration and activities. After this verbal lashing by God, we felt so very bad. We felt so filthy. We felt so hypocritical. We had disappointed our God. When we finally got back to Montgomery, Alabama and back into our house, God had us to get our Bible. He then showed us in the scriptures why he had rebuked us. He showed us why we should not have anything at all to do with Christmas and its associated activities. He led us to I Corinthians Chapter 10, Verses. 27 & 28 and I Corinthians Chapter 6, Verses. 15 – 18.

<u>I Corinthians Ch. 10 V. 27</u>
"If any of them that believe not bid you to a feast, and ye be disposed to go; whatsoever is set before you eat, asking no questions for conscience sake."

Here we see, that a so-called Christian or Christian/ Saint is allowed to eat with a sinner, heathen, unbeliever, if we so desire. Also, we see, that if we accept an invitation to eat, then we should eat the food offered to us and not reject it, which would result in hurting the feelings of the host. After God had us to read the above Scripture, then He told us to read the next verse.

<u>I Corinthians Ch. 10 V. 28</u>
"But if any man say unto you, this is offered in sacrifice unto idols, <u>eat not</u> for his sake that shewed it, and for conscience sake..."

Here we see, that if a sinner, heathen, unbeliever, and we might add, anyone else, invite us to eat food associated with idolatry, such as Christmas food, we should reject it, whether it hurts their feeling or not.

Eating the food associated with the idolatry of Christmas and Easter are two of the three main reasons why there are so many people sick and, even, dying. Most of, nearly all, of the churches participate in the communion ceremony. They take communion. The scriptures indicate if you take communion unworthily then you would get sick or even, die.

I Corinthians Ch. 11 V. 26 – 30
"For as often as you eat this bread, and drink this cup, ye do shew the Lord's death till he come. Wherefore whosoever shall eat this bread, and drink this cup unworthily shall be guilty of the body and the blood of the Lord. But let him eat that bread, and drink that cup. For he that eateth and drinketh unworthily, eateth and drinketh, damnation to himself, not discerning the Lord's body. For this cause many are weak and sickly among you, and many sleep."

If you eat the food associated with idolatry of Christmas and Easter, you are unworthy to take communion. This is additionally, indicated in the scriptures below.

<u>I Corinthians Ch. 10 Vs. 15 & 16</u>
"I speak as to wise men: judge ye what I say. The cup of blessings which we bless, is not the communion of the blood of Christ? The bread which we break, is it not the communion of the body of Christ?"

<u>I Corinthians Ch. 10 Vs. 20 & 21</u>
"But I say, that the things which the Gentiles sacrifice, they sacrifice to devils, and not to God: and I would not that ye should have fellowship with devils. Ye cannot drink of the cup of the Lord, and the cup of devils: ye cannot be partakers of the Lord's Table and of the table of devils."

Christmas food is a sacrifice to devils. Even sacrifice to Santa Claus. Even sacrifice to Satan.

We mentioned earlier, that eating Christmas and Easter food were two of three main reasons why some are sick and, even, dead when they take communion. The third main reason is participation in pastor's appreciation. These extravagant events honor the pastor as lords/gods. They also raise great sums of money for them. They, the pastor get credit for all the good things that God has done for the people. These appreciations are very great activities of idolatry. There are several reasons why these appreciations are despicable and abominable in God's sight. First of all, God's ministers are to be servants and not lord's over God's people.

<u>I Peter Ch. 5 Vs. 2-5</u>
"Feed the flock of God which is among you, taking the oversight thereof, not by constraint, but willingly; not for filthy lucre, but of a ready mind; neither as being lord's over God's heritage, but being ensamples of the flock. And when the chief Shepherd shall appear, ye shall receive a crown of glory that fadeth not away."

God spoke to us several years ago and said that those ministers that were having appreciations were receiving their regard. Interpretation, receiving their only reward.

Another reason why these appreciations are despicable and abominable to God, is that these pastors should not be taking the credit for something that God has done. They even have the people praising them for things that have not even taken place. Speaking lies of praises. Lies of praying. Lies of healings that never took place. Lies of devils being cast out that never happened. Lies of teaching the truth when in fact they taught lies. Lies of salvation when actually the people are being deceived by them into hell. Other lies. Even if the above things were not lies, the pastors should not be getting credit for God's doings.

Another reason that their appreciations are despicable and abominable to God, is the raising of these great sums of money for the pastors. First of all, they probably did not deserve anything. But even if they actually had done the work of God, God has already declared in the scriptures how they are to be compensated. Their compensation is to be through the regular collection of part of the tithes and offerings.

With this pastor appreciation idolatry there is, also in most cases, a related meal. This is a food sacrifice of idolatry. Whether this is at the church, a restaurant, someone's house, etc., it is a food sacrifice of idolatry. You might not have had anything to do with anything else related to the appreciation, but if you either ate, bought something, served or did anything else related to this food, you would be a partaker of this food sacrifice idolatry. Then, if you take communion, you are in jeopardy of damnation. You are in jeopardy of being weak, sickly and death.

Let us get back to our original discussion. Let us continue with what God showed us in the scriptures of I Corinthians of why He rebuked us for participating in the Christmas associated activities in Mobile, Alabama.

II Corinthians Ch. 6, V. 15
"And what concord hath Christ with Belial? Or what part hath he that believeth with an infidel?"

Belial is a Satanic or demonic person. Infidel is an unbeliever of God's word. The above scripture, therefore, means that a Christian/Saint should not have fellowship with a sinners, heathens, unbelievers, in their idolatrous religious functions or activities. We should not be having so-called praise and worship together during such as Christmas' programs.

II Corinthians Ch. 6, V. 16
"And what agreement hath the temple of God with idols? For ye are the temple of the living God; as God hath said, I WILL DWELL IN THEM, AND WALK IN THEM; AND I WILL BE THEIR GOD, AND THEY SHALL BE MY PEOPLE."

Here we see, that God says, that a Christian/ Saint is his Temple that he dwells in. God says that it is contradictory for idol worshippers to be worshipping with his Temple. Idols are worshipped by the world as if they are God. As we showed earlier, God says that those that worship him must worship in truth. God says in his word that you cannot serve to masters.

Luke Ch. 16, V.13
"No servant can serve two masters; for either he will hate the one, and love the other; or else he will hold to the one, and despise the other. Ye cannot serve God and mammon."

This is why when we tell people the truth about Christmas, some actually hate us for doing so. They want to hold on to Christmas, even, if it means going against the word of God. When the truth is told you of the word, and you hate the person for telling you, you are actually hating God.

John Ch. 15, V. 18
"If the world hate you, ye know that it hated me before it hated you."

John Ch. 15, V. 19
"If ye were of the world, the world would love his own: but because ye are not of the world, but I have chosen you out of the world, therefore the world hatheth you."

II Corinthians Ch. 6, V. 17
"WHEREFORE COME OUT FROM AMONG THEM AND BE YE SEPARATE, SAITH THE LORD, AND

TOUCH NOT THE UNCLEAN THING; AND I WILL RECEIVE YOU..."

Here we see, clearly, that God does not want his people to be involved with the idolatrous activities and associations of Christmas. No matter the pretence, that they/you are serving God. Additionally, God say, if you leave that idolatrous abomination alone, that you can be his servant.

<u>II Corinthians Ch. 6, V. 18</u>
"AND WILL BE A FATHER UNTO YOU, AND YE SHALL BE MY SONS AND DAUGHTERS, saith the Lord Almighty."

The only time that a saint should have any Church related fellowship with sinners is when he or she is ministering to the sinners; when he or she is trying to get them saved.

You might say, I celebrate Christmas and I am a son/ daughter of God. You might say, I have been born again/saved. That, I have been born of water and of the Spirit. Well, it might be so, but if you reject these words, that we have written and will write, in this book, God will withdraw his Spirit from you and you will go the way of idolaters. You will go to hell and burn in the lake of fire.

We will now address giving Christmas gifts. You

say, this show love. This is not a true show of love. To prove it, just ask whom ever wants to give you a gift on Christmas to wait and give it to you in February or March; without any Christmas cards or wrapping associated with it; without any reference to Christmas. You will see, that come February and March, you will not receive the gift. Even if it is something that they know you need. The desire to give you a gift is nothing more than their hypocritical show of love, to be partakers with you in the idolatrous Christmas extravaganza. Even if it was true love, all love is not good. All love is not good! Remember?

<u>I John Ch. 2, V. 15</u>
"Love not the world, neither the things that are in the world. If any man love the world, the love of the Father is not in him."

The world's time on the clock to the end is rushing toward zero. The world is coming to an end. Refer to our Book "When the End Will Come." In these last days, the idolatrous (Anti-Christ) Beast, Abomination of Desolation, will be worshipped on this earth as God. During this time when God's servants are killed, the people of the world will rejoice and give and receive gifts because of their deaths. Could this be Christmas time? At this time, God will come back to get his people/saints off this earth. This has been called the rapture, the first resurrection. God will then bring wrath upon those that are left on earth. They will, also, go to hell and burn in the lake of fire. All will go to hell and the lake of fire, except those very, very, few of them that will go into the (1000) one thousand year millennium that might, could, get saved.

Revelation Ch.11, V. 8
"And their dead bodies shall lie in the street of the great city..."

Revelation Ch.11, V. 10
"And they that dwell upon the earth shall rejoice over them, and make merry, and shall send gifts one to another..."

This time of sending and receiving gifts, is similar to the Christmas season. JESUS did say that when he would comeback, it would be such a time on earth of celebration and rejoicing.

Matthew Ch. 24, Vs. 37-39
"But as the days of Noe were, so shall also the coming of the son of man be. For as in the days that were before the flood they were eating and drinking, marrying and giving in marriage, until the day that Noe entered in the ark. And knew not until the flood came, and took them all away; so shall also the coming o the Son of man be."

The above scriptures refer to JESUS as the Son of man.

[Note This. This is an insert to this Book just before it was published. In the above scripture JESUS said when he comes back that people will be "marrying and giving marriage." People always have been marrying and giving in marriage. God gave me a revelation on January, 2013, as we call it, that this marrying and giving a marriage were referring to that of sodomites/homosexuals, men marrying men and women marrying women.]

You might at this point, and should at this point, say Ok, Ok, Ok, I believe you! But, what about what you said in the "INTRODUCTION" of the book? You said, you can, you believe you can, tell us the day when JESUS was born. You might say, I am ready to hear it.

As we have shown, JESUS was born in the month Adar. Adar, as we have said, this Jewish and Biblical month, is in our month of March.

To understand why we believe that we know the day JESUS was born in the month of Adar, let us first consider certain questions. The very first question is why not? You cannot come up with a good answer.

Second question, if the Holy Bible tells of JESUS' death why not tell of his birth? The Bible let us know the exact day when JESUS was crucified. The Bible tells us that JESUS was crucified on the (14th) fourteenth day of the month Abib, the Passover.

<u>Exodus Ch. 12, Vs. 1 & 2</u>
"And the LORD spake unto Moses and Aaron in the land of Egypt saying, this month shall be unto you the beginning of months: it shall be the <u>first month</u> of the year to you."

We have shown earlier that this first month is the month <u>Abib</u>. Refer to Deuteronomy Chapter 16, Verse 1. Also, refer to Exodus Chapter 13, Verse 4.

<u>Exodus Ch. 13, V. 4</u>
"This day came we out in the month Abib."

<u>Exodus Ch. 12, V. 3</u>
"Speak ye unto all the congregation of Israel, saying in the tenth day of this month they shall take to them every man a lamb for an house."

This lamb was the symbolic representation of JESUS.

<u>Exodus Ch. 12, Vs. 5-7</u>
"Your lamb shall be without blemish, a male of the first year: ye shall take it out from the sheep, or

from the goats: And ye shall keep it up until the fourteenth day of the same month: and the whole assembly of the congregation of Israel shall kill it in the evening. And they shall take of the blood, and strike it on the two side posts and on the upper door post of the houses, wherein they shall eat it."

The above scriptures, as said earlier, show that JESUS was crucified on the fourteenth (14th) day of the month Abib. Therefore, Easter, which changes from month to month from date to date, could not be when JESUS was resurrected. Like Christmas, Easter is an idolatrous abominable event, worshipping an idol god. Refer to our Book "JESUS WAS NOT CRUCIFIED WHEN AS HAS BEEN TAUGHT".

Let us leave Easter alone and get back to the birth of JESUS. Let us get back to the question of whether there is a reason, why the birthday of JESUS would not be in the Holy Bible? Well, we really do not have to keep on with this line of questions. The reason is, because, in fact the Holy Bible made great effort for us to know the birthday of JESUS. God, even sent an angel to tell of JESUS' birthday.

Luke Ch. 2, Vs. 7-11
"And she brought forth her firstborn son, and wrapped him in swaddling clothes, and laid him

in a manger; because there was no room for them in the inn. And there were in the same country shepherds abiding in the field, keeping watch over their flock by night. And, lo, the angel of the Lord shone round about them: and they were sore afraid. And the angel said unto them, fear not: for, behold, I bring you good tiding of great joy, which shall be to all people. <u>For unto you is born this day in the City of David, a Saviour, which is Christ the Lord.</u>"

It is evident then that God wanted us to know exactly when JESUS, his Son, was born. God knew that those shepherds, who the angel appeared to, would be telling everyone, who would listen of this extraordinary, long looked for, event. Refer to Luke Chapter 2, Verse 17. God knew that those who the shepherds told would tell others. God wanted this glorious good news to spread over the entire earth. Also, God knew that Satan would, use the Pope and Constantine to, tell the lie that JESUS was born on Christmas. God wanted us, his saints, to be able to expose his lie. We then know that there must be someway to verify the day when JESUS was born. The Catholic Church and the Pope(s) had killed all of the true saints of God who would not go along their Christmas lie. So thorough were their efforts, until, now in these days, no one was left to tell the truth of when JESUS was born. NOTE THIS. It is about (10) ten to (20) twenty books that have been taken out of the Holy Bible by the Catholic Church and maybe others. We believe that in at least one of those books, it would have shown very clearly that Christmas was not when JESUS WAS BORN. For example, the scriptures mention the Books of Nathan and Gad, but there are no Books of Nathan and Gad in the Holy Bible.

I Chronicles Ch. 29, V. 29

"Now the acts of David the king, first and last, behold, they are written in the book of Samuel the seer, and in book of Nathan the prophet, and in the book of Gad the seer."

But there has to be somewhere in the scriptures that point to this birthday of JESUS. We believe that we have found this scriptural location.

Luke Ch.2,Vs. 15, 16 & 17

"...the shepherds said one to another; Let us now go even unto Bethlehem, and see this thing which is come to pass, which the Lord hath made known unto us. And they came with haste, and found Mary, and Joseph and the babe lying in a manger. And when they had seen it, they made known abroad the saying which was told them concerning the child."

Before we go any further, you must remember what God says that the months are not what you say, the world says, that the months are. You must remember that God's twelve months of the year; do not coincide with your, the world's, twelve months.

You must understand that God says that there are 30 days of the month for all twelve months. This means, according to God, that there are three hundred and sixty (360) days in a year. You, the world, say(s) that there can be either 28, 29,30 Or 31 days to a month. This means, according to you, the world, that there can be either(365) three hundred and sixty-five or (366) three hundred and thirty-six days in a year.

<u>Note</u>: Even the present day Jewish Calendar is not as God says the months and days should be.

Man, evidently, must think that he is more intelligent than God, even though, God made the days and months. Even though God made man. We have shown the difference of what God says, about the months and days, and what, you say or the world says, about the months and days, in several of our books that we have written. One of those books is our Book "When the End Will Come".

We, again, will show what God says about the months and days.

Daniel Ch.7, V. 25

"And he shall speak great words against the most High, and shall wear out the saints of the most High, and think to change times and laws: and they shall be given into his hand until <u>a time</u> and <u>times</u> and the <u>dividing of time</u>."

As we will show later, <u>time</u> is equal to <u>one year</u>, <u>times</u> equal <u>two years</u> and <u>dividing of time</u> equal <u>to (1/2) half of a year, six months.</u>

Daniel Ch.12, Vs. 6 & 7

"... How long shall it be to the end of these wonders?... it shall be for <u>a time, times</u>, and <u>an half</u>; and when he shall have accomplished to scatter the power of the holy people, all these things shall be finished."

In the above scripture, time and the times are one (1) and two (2) years, respectively as was in the previous scripture.

In the previous scripture Daniel Chapter 7, Verse 25, <u>(1/2) one-half of a year, six months</u> were called the <u>dividing of time</u>. In the above scripture, Daniel Chapter 12, Verse 7, <u>six months</u> is called "<u>an half</u>."

In both of the scriptural references of the Book

of Daniel, Chapter 7 and Chapter 12, the periods of time referred, are the same. This is the three and one-half (3 ½) year reign of the so-called Anti-Christ. Time, times and the dividing of time equals three and one-half (3 ½) years. This period is called the Great Tribulation. The Anti-Christ, so-called, will be an evil person on this earth possessed by Satan. He will be Satan's body on earth. He is Pope John Paul II. Refer to our Book "The Name of the (Anti-Christ) Beast and 666 Identification."

The Biblical names for Anti-Christ are:

1. Little Horn
2. Vile Person
3. Abomination of Desolation
4. King of Fierce Countenance
5. Son of Perdition
6. Man of Sin
7. Beast

Let us get back to the of defining of the days of the months.

<u>Revelation Ch.11, Vs. 2& 3</u>
"... and the holy city will be tread under foot forty <u>and two months</u>. And I will give power unto my two witnesses, and they shall prophesy <u>a thousand two hundred and threescore days</u>, clothed in sackcloth."

The above scriptures are also referring to the period of the reign of the so-called Anti-Christ. Here we see that three and one- half (3 ½) years, equals forty-two (42) months, which are equal to one thousand two hundred and sixty (1,260) days. That means a year is equal to three hundred and sixty (360) days. The math is <u>1,260 ÷360 =3 ½.</u> The math is 42 x 30= 1,260; 1,260 days. 3 ½ years, 42 months. This mean a year equals 360 days. At <u>twelve months a year</u>, this means that <u>a month</u> equal <u>thirty (30) days.</u> Further evidence of this truth can be seen in the following scriptures. These are scriptures of the three and one-half (3 ½) years reign of the so-called Anti-Christ. The Great Tribulation period.

<u>Revelation Ch.12, V. 6</u>
"And the woman fled into the wilderness, where she hath a place prepared of God, that they should feed her there<u> a thousand two hundred and threescore days."</u>

A thousand two hundred and threescore days = 1260 days.

<u>Revelation Ch. 12, V. 14</u>
"And to the woman were given two wings of a great eagle, that she might fly into the wilderness, into her place where she is nourished for a time,

and times and half a time from the face of the serpent."

Like before, time equals one (1) year, times equal two years and half equals six months.

<u>Revelation Ch.13, V. 4 &5</u>
"And they worshipped the dragon which gave power unto the beast: and the worshipped the beast saying, who is like unto the beast? Who is able to make war with him? And there was given unto him a mouth speaking great things and blasphemies; and power was given unto him to continue forty and two months."

we have shown and confirmed with the scriptures, that <u>a month</u> equals to <u>thirty (30) days</u>.

You must keep this in mind as we discuss the things to come that the months will be thirty (30) days. You cannot use a present day Calendar. Neither, even, can you use the present day Jewish Calendar. The present day Jewish Calendar has been changed, also, to show that they, also are more knowledgeable than God. Even God's chosen people, the Jews, have evidently, concluded that God does not know what he is talking about. No matter, that God created the universe.

The error and audacity, even, the indignity and

ignorance, of man, are why we are behind in time. Literally behind time. Satan has blinded us. We say that it is the year, 2003, when actually, according to God, it is the year 2032. Yes, the year 2032 A.D. Refer to our Books "The Big Lie" and "When the End Will Come".

Satan can only succeed through ignorance. Idol god worshippers are included in this ignorant number. Christmas participations and associated activities of God's people/saints are among this number, the ignorant.

Hosea Ch.4, V. 6
"My people are destroyed for lack of knowledge ..."

Now we can go to see when JESUS was born.

We will first tell you the day that we believe to be the birthday of JESUS, then we will explain. Before we go further, think about this. Would not the very special event of the birth of the Son of God, be associated with some very special event and would not this event be in the Scriptures of both the Old and New Testaments? We believe that JESUS was born on the same day of the month that Moses saw the burning bush that would not burn up. It seems very appropriate for this to be so. This is the day that God gave the word to Moses for the deliverance/ salvation of his people from the bondage of slavery from Egypt. Well, JESUS was given by the Father for the deliverance/salvation of all the world from the bondage of Satan. Also, you must remember that JESUS is called the Word.

<u>John Ch.1,Vs. 1 & 14</u>
"In the beginning was the <u>Word</u>, and the <u>Word</u> was with God, and the <u>Word</u> was God. And the <u>Word</u> was made <u>flesh</u>, and dwelt among us, (and we beheld his glory, as of the <u>only begotten of the Father</u>) full of grace and truth."

So, we see that Moses received the <u>word</u> to get Israel, God's people, delivered/saved from bondage. In like manner, we see the "<u>Word</u>", JESUS, given to deliver/save from bondage.

There were several things of the Old Testament of the Holy Bible that were symbolic representations of JESUS. As we have seen, the Passover lamb being without blemish represented JESUS.

<u>Colossians Ch. 2, Vs. 16 & 17</u>
"...an holy day...the Sabbath days...are a shadow of things to come; but the body is of Christ."

<u>Hebrews Ch. 10, Vs. 1 & 7</u>
"For the law having a shadow of good things to come...LO, I COME (IN THE VOLUME OF THE BOOK IT IS WRITTEN OF ME,) TO DO THY WILL, O GOD."

The ark that Noah built was a symbolic representation of JESUS. The Ark of the Covenant was also symbolically representing JESUS. Some have characterized these symbolic representations as "a type of JESUS". It is not our preference to use this phraseology. We have thus for spoken of things and a lamb as symbolically representing JESUS, but JESUS was also symbolically represented by people. The most notable one was, Moses in delivering the children of Israel from the bondage of slavery out of Egypt. God even said that he used Moses as a god.

Exodus Ch. 7, V. 1
"And the <u>LORD</u> said unto Moses, see, I have made thee <u>a god</u> to Pharaoh: and Aaron thy bother shall be thy prophet."

Moses status of a symbolic representation of JESUS was so perfect, that Moses even dared to say that <u>JESUS</u>, the Son of God, would be like him.

Deuteronomy Ch. 18, V. 15
"The LORD thy God will raise up unto thee a Prophet from the midst of thee, of thy brethren, <u>like unto me</u>: unto him ye shall hearken..."

Not only did Moses, dare to say that JESUS would be like him, but God, himself, said it.

<u>Deuteronomy Ch. 18, V. 18</u>
"I will raise them up a Prophet from among their brethren, <u>like unto thee</u>, and will put my words in his mouth; and he shall speak unto them all that I shall command him."

Since <u>Moses</u> was such a perfect symbolic representation of <u>JESUS</u>, then, it is very likely, that the <u>day</u> that Moses was to become a deliverer/savior like unto JESUS, would be the same day of <u>JESUS' birth</u>.

We have said that JESUS was born in the month Adar which is March. We will now show, in the scriptures, that when Moses saw the burning bush he received the <u>word</u> of deliverance/salvation from God in the month Adar. Adar the twelfth month. This is when <u>Moses first</u> became a deliverer/savior <u>like unto JESUS.</u>

<u>NOTE</u>:
As always, Satan is a counterfeit. The true God's son was born on the true twelfth month of the year, the month Adar. The counterfeit, idol god, the lie, is said to be born on the world's twelfth month of the year, the month December.

Let us now prove our assertion about Moses and the burning bush. Let us go to the Old Testament of the Holy Bible.

For background we give this. In the days of Israel's four hundred (400) year slavery in Egypt, a certain king of Egypt gave a decree to have all the male babies of the Israelites killed. The king was god like to the Egyptians and called Pharaoh. When the killing decree was given a certain woman hid her baby from this slaughter. This baby was Moses.

NOTE:

Moses' life as a baby was spared/protected when a decree was given by a king to kill all the male babies. Also. JESUS' life as a baby was spared/protected when a decree was given by a king to kill the male babies.

Exodus Ch. 1, V. 15

"And the king of Egypt spake to the Hebrew midwives...And he said, When ye do the office of a midwife to the Hebrew women, and see them upon the stools; if it be a son, then ye shall kill him: but if it be a daughter, then she shall live."

Matthew Ch. 2, V. 16

"Then, Herod...sent forth, and slew all the children, that were in Bethlehem, and in all the coast thereof, from two years old and under..."

God had it be so that Pharaoh, himself, ended up raising up this baby and child. Unknowingly, he raised up this baby and child. He did not know that the baby was supposed to be one of his decreed victims. He did not know that Moses was an Israeli slave child. God had it to be worked out that Moses own mother nursed him and trained him as a child. Moses, therefore, knew who he was and his Jewish heritage. Note This. JESUS, also, was a baby in Egypt.

<u>Matthew Ch. 2, V. 13</u>
"...behold, the angel of the Lord appeareth to Joseph in a dream, saying, Arise, and take the young child and his mother, and flee into Egypt, and be thou there until I give the word..."

This was the young child JESUS.

When Moses was grown, then forty years old, he killed an Egyptian because he was beating an Israeli slave. He had to flee from Egypt from Pharaoh's wrath. Moses went to a place across a desert to a place called Midian. There he married an Ethiopian wife. When Moses was (80) eighty years old, there appeared an unusual thing in his sight. As he drew near, he saw that it was a bush on fire, but the bush would never burn away. Then all of a sudden, Moses was really astonished. A voice came out of the fire. God told Moses to take his shoes off for the ground that he was standing on was holy ground. God then gave Moses the <u>word</u> to get his people delivered out of bondage.

<u>Exodus Ch. 3, Vs. 1 & 2</u>
"Now Moses kept the flock of Jethro his father-in-law, the priest of Midian: and he led the flock to the backside of the desert, and came to the mountain of God, even to Horeb. And the angel of the LORD appeared unto him in a flame of fire out of the midst of a bush: and he looked, and, behold, the bush burned with fire, and the bush was not consumed."

<u>Exodus Ch. 3, Vs. 4 & 5</u>
"And when the LORD saw that he turned aside to see, God, called unto him out of the midst of the bush, and said, Moses, Moses. And he said, here am I. And he said, draw not nigh hither: put off thy shoes from off thy feet, for the place whereon thou standest is holy ground."

<u>NOTE</u>:
In all of the appearances of God to people in the Holy Bible, this is the only time when God required any to take off their shoes. We believe that God said so, at this time, because of the significance of this day being the birthday of JESUS, the Son of God.

After God had told Moses to take off his shoes. God told Moses the purpose of this great encounter. God gave him the <u>word</u> for deliverance/salvation of his people from bondage.

<u>Exodus Ch.3, V. 10</u>
"Come now therefore, and I will send thee unto Pharaoh, that thou mayest bring forth my people the children of Israel out of Egypt."

After some encouragement and persuasion by God, Moses headed on his way to Egypt with the <u>word</u> from God to Pharaoh.

<u>NOTE</u>:
This word was no ordinary word. This was a word from God. A word that God spoke. When we speak it is just a sound. When God speaks things are created, things are manifested. In the beginning, the Bible tells us, God spoke the universe in existence. Therefore, this word of deliverance/salvation of his people had to bring forth results. Before Moses went to carry out his mission, God told him that he would cause Pharaoh to be stubborn toward his word so that Egypt could be punished with plagues. Its due judgment for the great evil that it had done against his people, Israel. When Moses would eventually get to Egypt, he told Pharaoh that God said let his people go. As

would be expected, Pharaoh said no. God used Moses to afflict Pharaoh and Egypt with plagues until Pharaoh would eventually let the people of God go.

The days that it took Moses to leave from Midian until the day before Pharaoh was finally persuaded/ forced to let God's people go, was twenty-three (23) days. The Passover was when Pharaoh let the people go. In the beginning Moses told Pharaoh that God said let his people go. As would be expected, Pharaoh said no. On subsequent trips to Pharaoh for the same purpose, God used Moses to afflict Pharaoh and Egypt with plagues until Pharaoh would eventually let the people of God go.

The days that it took Moses to leave from Midian until the day before Pharaoh was finally persuaded/ forced to let God's people go, was twenty-three days. The Passover was when Pharaoh was forced to let the people go. This ensures that this time of the Month of Adar would be in March. Twenty-three days before the Passover would be in March. For conservation of time, we show our derivation of the twenty-three (23) days using a sort of chronological summary of events. We provide you with the day(s) that is associated with the particular event. The following is how we justify our assertion of twenty-three (23) days.

Days before the Passover after God told Moses to go to Egypt and tell Pharaoh to let his people go:

1. Journey to Egypt: _____ 3 days
   (Exodus Ch. 3, V. 8 & Ch. 5, V. 3)
2. First Defiance of Pharaoh resulting in day(s) of bricks making without straw before Moses next visit; _____ 1 day
   (Exodus Ch. 5, Vs. 1 & 14)
3. Moses rod became a serpent _____ 1 day
   (Exodus Ch.7, Vs. 10-13)
4. Water turned into blood _____ 7 days
   (Exodus Ch.7, Vs. 15-20 & 21-25)
5. Plague of frogs_____ 1 day
6. Plague of Lice_____ 1 day
   (Exodus Ch. 8, Vs. 16-19)
7. Plague of flies warning_____ 1 day
   (Exodus Ch. 8, V.20)
8. Plague of flies_____ 1 day
   (Exodus Ch.8, Vs. 22-28 & 32)
9. Cattle, horses, assets, camels, oxen, and sheep death plague _____ 1 day
   (Exodus Ch. 9, Vs. 1 & 5-7)
10. Plague of boil with blains_____ 1 day
    (Exodus Ch. 9, Vs. 8-12)
11. Plague of hail _____ 1 day
    (Exodus Ch. 9, Vs. 13, 18, 22, 27, 28 & 34)
12. Plagues of locusts _____ 1 day

(Exodus Ch. 10, Vs. 10, Vs. 1-4, 12 & 16-20)

13. Plague of darkness_____3 days

    (Exodus Ch. 10, Vs. 21 & 24-29)

    TOTAL DAYS _____23 days

14. Plague of firstborn death <u>14th of Abib, Passover</u>

To find out the day that Moses saw the burning bush, we need only to go back (23) twenty-three days before the Passover. Go back (23) twenty-three days before the (14th) fourteenth of the month Abib. <u>Remember,</u> all of the months, according to God, have (30) thirty days. The result of this back counting puts Moses' burning bush experience on the <u>(20th) twentieth </u>day of the <u>month before Abib.</u> This is the <u>(20th) twentieth day </u>of the <u>month Adar.</u> Understand this. That the first day of each Biblical month begins with a new moon.

<u>I Samuel Ch. 20, Vs. 24, 25 & 27</u>

"...and when the <u>new moon </u>was come, the King sat him down to eat meat. And the king sat upon his seat, as at other times, even upon a seat by the wall: and Jonathan arose, and Abner sat by Saul's side, and David's place was empty. And it came to pass on the morrow, which was the <u>second day of the month</u>, that David's place was empty: and Saul said unto Jonathan his son, Wherefore cometh not the son of Jesse to meat, neither yesterday, nor today?"

When our month of March begins on the new moon, then March's days will line up with Adar's days. JESUS, the Son of God, was born on the (20th) twentieth day of the month of Adar. On our leap years, the (20th) twentieth day of March is the beginning of Spring. When our month of March is a day before this new moon, then we call March (21ST) twenty-first Spring. This will be either the (20th) twentieth or (21st) twenty-first day of March, depending on whether March is aligned with the new moon. We believe that this the (20th) twentieth of Adar is the true day of the beginning of Spring. Spring the new birth. JESUS WOULD HAVE BEEN BORN ON THE 20th DAY OF ADAR WHICH WE BELIEVE TO BE GOD's TRUE (1ST) FIRST DAY OF SPRING.

NOTE THIS. When Moses saw the burning bush he was with the sheep eating green grass out in the field.

Exodus Ch. 3, Vs. 1 & 2

"And Moses kept the flock of Jethro his father in law, the priest of Midian: and he led the flock to the backside of the desert, and came to the mountain of God, even to Hored. And the angel of the LORD appeared unto him in a flame of fire out of the midst of a bush: and he looked, and behold, the bush burned with fire, and the bush was not consumed."

It was not winter. It was not December. It was not December (25) twenty-fifth. It was not Christmas. It was the Month of Adar. It was the (20TH) twentieth day of the Month of Adar. It was the Month of March.

Hosea Ch. 4, V.6
"My people are destroyed for lack of knowledge..."

John Ch. 8, V. 32
"And ye shall know the truth and the truth shall make you free."

As a side note:
Prophetess Sylvia Franklin, my wife, was born on March (20th) twentieth. Our son Elijah Jeremiah Ezekiel Franklin was scheduled to be on March (20th) twentieth, but was born premature. Our daughter Rebekah Anna Franklin was scheduled to be born on March (20th) twentieth, but was born about two weeks early.

APOSTLE FREDERICK E. FRANKLIN'S TESTIMONY

Let me give you my personal testimony. Let me tell you about how I got filled with the Holy Ghost. Back in 1985 I lived in Washington, D.C. I was not married at that time. It was in October of 1985. I had my own business as a Utilities Engineering Consultant. As a sinner and as usually was the case, I left out of a certain bar around 1:00 am. When finally I reached the place where I was living and was opening my door, the telephone began to ring. I went in and answered the telephone. It was my first cousin calling from Mobile, Alabama. He, also, was about high and was just getting in from a bar. As usually was the case, we started talking about God. We knew little to nothing about God, but somehow we always started talking about God. As we talked, I started talking about the preachers of God. I said that those O lying preachers that say they lay hands on people and they get healed are the worst ones. I said only Jesus could heal someone like that. I at least knew that Jesus could heal like that. My cousin said you are right. Two drunks talking. He then said the only other ones who could do that were Peter, John, Paul and the other Apostles of the Holy Bible. I was shocked. I was so shocked that I got sober. I said what! What! He said yes! Peter, John, Paul and the other Apostles laid hands on the people and they got healed. I was totally astounded! I was totally amazed! I was sober!

After we hanged up the telephone, I went and picked up the Bible which I had kept with me since about 1963. I had never opened the Bible I was just religious and kept it with me. I had been putting off reading it for all these years. When the urge would come to me to read it, I would put it off to the next month, or next week, or next day, or when I finished a certain project, or when I finished during this or that. I did not know it then, but I know now, the urge was God trying to get me to read the Bible. I finally dusted off and opened that Bible. It was now around 2:00 am. I wanted to see for myself where it said that a man could lay hands on a person and he or she could get healed. I was after all, an Electrical Engineer and this was illogical. How could flesh, blood and bones heal someone? It did not make any sense. Not having any idea where to look, I searched and searched and searched. I read and read and read. Finally, somewhere between 3:00-4:00 am, I found it. I saw that Peter laid hands on people and they got healed. It was amazing! It was like a very bright light was turned on in my head. I was speechless. To understand the greatness of my astonishment, you need to understand my childhood hopelessness. I, as a child, being black brought up in Alabama, living far out in a rural area, started working when I was four years old. I would go outside of our house at night, walking through the woods, looking up in the sky at the moon and the stars, and ask God why? I knew it had to be a God. I would ask God why would he leave his children down on this earth at the mercy of Satan? Satan of course, I knew, had no mercy. I could not understand why. Everything that seemed to be good, appeared to be on Satan's side. The evil people had it. White folks had it who were doing evil. Why, why, why, was my question? I never received an answer. It appeared that God could care less about the suffering of and in justice to his children on this earth.

When I saw that someone could get healed by another just by laying hands on them, then I understood clearly the answer to my why. I understood that God had not left us at the mercy of Satan. I, however, wanted to see could anyone lay hands on people and they could get healed. As I continued to search and read, now about day break, I "discovered" that you had to have the Holy Ghost to be able to heal. I wanted then to see could anyone receive the Holy Ghost. Now far in the morning of the next day, I "discovered" that anyone could receive the Holy Ghost. I "discovered" that you spoke in tongues when you received the Holy Ghost. My life desire would never be the same again. I wanted to see how I could receive the Holy Ghost. I learned that you had to repent. So, I asked God to forgive my sins. Then I ask God to give me the Holy Ghost, let me speak in tongues. Nothing happened. I did not speak in tongues. All that day I was asking God to forgive my sins and to let me speak in tongues. I did not work that day. This went on all day and into the night. Nothing ever happened. Exhausted I fell asleep into the next morning. When I woke the next day I started doing the same thing. I asked God to forgive my sins and let me speak in tongues. Nothing happened. I thought that maybe I need to read God's word and then I might receive the Holy Ghost. So, I read several Books of the Bible. Then I asked God to forgive my sins and let me speak in tongues. Nothing happened. I did this over and over each day and nothing ever happened. I had stop working all together. To receive the Holy Ghost was the most important thing in my life. I made a pledge to God that I would not go to the bars again. Nothing happened as I sought for the Holy Ghost. I made a pledge to God to stop drinking and stop smoking marijuana. Nothing happened. I made a pledge to God to stop fornicating. Nothing happened as I sought for the Holy Ghost. I was praying for the Holy Ghost and reading God's word and nothing happened. I decided to read the whole Bible. I read from Genesis through the Book of Revelation and nothing happened as I sought for the Holy Ghost during that time. Now it was the end of the year of 1985 and nothing happened as I sought for the Holy Ghost. I decided to move from Washington, D.C., back to my house in Montgomery, Alabama. Now after reading the whole Bible, I was praying about (22) twenty two hours a day to receive the Holy Ghost and nothing happened. I started crying and praying and nothing happened. I had only cried (4) four times in my life. I remember all the way back from (2) two years old. Crying and seeking for the Holy Ghost is all I did. I never spoke in tongues. This crying and seeking God for the Holy Ghost reached now into August of the year 1986. I had counted all of the months, weeks, and days to that time of seeking for the Holy Ghost, now seeking about (22) twenty two hours a day. I had about (3) three months before, cleaned out my house of everything that I thought was sinful. I threw away all pornography, whiskey, wine and beer, marijuana and whatever I thought was sinful into my trash can. I did this and nothing ever happened. Now here it was in August, seeking to speak in tongues and I had not. I said, I thought, that maybe I need to join a Church. This might would help, I thought. I looked into the yellow pages of the phone book and chose (4) four churches that I would check out to join. This was now August 3, 1986. I was still seeking God for the Holy Ghost. I still was crying and praying to speak in tongues about (22) twenty two hours a day. On August 3, 1986, I turned on my television early in the morning and turning the channels I saw and heard some ridiculous sounding Church Choir singing with the TV camera shaking. I stopped to see what in the world would this be on television so unprofessional. I was amazed. I had once worked at a television station in Cleveland, Ohio, and I was just amazed at this. As I looked and listened in amazement, a young woman came before the camera to introduce/present her Apostle. She said that her Apostle laid hands on people, preformed many miracles and prayed for many to receive the Holy Ghost. This really caught my attention. I thought, could this be the answer to my quest? Then her Apostle came forth. A black, tall, old man, Apostle William A. Tumlin. I had already decided that I wanted to join a church under an old man who really knew something about God. Also, I wanted it to be a small church. I did not want anything to be like that Baptist Church that I was brought up in. All they cared about was looks, a big choir, a big church, a big funeral, always looks. They cared about looks, but yet certain ones was committing adultery and it seemed to be alright. Many were drunks and it seemed not to matter. I was brought up in this and had not learned hardly anything that I had finally read in the Bible.

Yet seeking God for the Holy Ghost, on August 10, 1986, I decided to first check out this Church and Apostle that I had seen on Television, before checking out the other churches. I went to the Church and it was a small church. I went into the Church and the Apostle preached and ask did anyone want to join the Church, I to my amazement went up and join the Church. I thought that the Apostle would pray for me to receive the Holy Ghost, but he did not. I was confused. After the service was dismissed, I went to the Apostle's wife and told her that I wanted to receive the Holy Ghost. She said, Oh, I thought you already had the Holy Ghost. She told me to go and tell the Apostle. I went to the Apostle and said I want to receive the Holy Ghost. He said Oh, I thought you already had the Holy Ghost. He said come back, either next Sunday or that afternoon before the 6:00 taping of the radio broadcast, and he would pray for me to receive the Holy Ghost. I said that I would come back before the taping of the broadcast. I was not about to wait for a whole week. I could tell you how many months, weeks and days I had been seeking for the Holy Ghost. I had been seeking for the Holy Ghost every day since October of 1985 and it was now August 10, 1986.

When I went home from Apostle Tumlin's Church, The All Nations Church of God, I did something that was key to me receiving the Holy Ghost. Remember I told you that I threw away all, pornography, whiskey, wine, beer, marijuana and other things I thought was sinful into my trash can. Well, I went back to my trash can and I got (2) two marijuana joints out of it and brought them back into my house. I had stop smoking marijuana during my time of seeking the Holy Ghost and had no intentions of smoking anymore. I did not know it at that time, but I know it now, it was Satan that convinced me to get those (2) two joints out of my trash can. I thought, Satan told me, that I might need them if I got a headache. I just had them in my closet in case I might need them for a headache. The Devil, Satan, just made a fool out of me. The only time I had those headaches is when I had a hangover. I was not going to have hangover because I had stop drinking. What a fool. However, on August, 10, 1986, before I went back to receive the Holy

Ghost, it had to be God who told me, I went to my closet and got those two joints and flushed them down my toilet stool. When I did this, it felt like a very, very, heavy weight was taken off me. At 5:00 on August 10, 1986, I was back at Apostle Tumlin's Church, The All Nations Church of God, to receive the Holy Ghost. I went in the Church and sat down in about the fourth row of the pews, next to the aisle, on the left side looking from the pulpit. There were about (3) three to (4) four people in the sanctuary, including the Apostle's wife. They were there praying. However, the Apostle was nowhere to be seen. I sat there waiting for the Apostle and he never showed up. It was now 5:30 pm and there was no sign of the Apostle. I was getting very anxious because the radio broadcast's taping was to start at 6:00 pm. Finally, the Apostle came out of a room from the front of the Church. I was so excited! I finally was going to receive the Holy Ghost! The Apostle walked towards me and down the aisle and right by me and went into the rest room near the entrance to the Church. He did not say one word to me. Not even a gesture toward me. Some minutes past by and he was still back there. I just kept praying. I just kept repenting. Finally he came out. He came to the back of me and put his hands on my head and said receive the Holy Ghost. I was excited and nervous. I did not know what to expect. Then with his hands on my head, he said speak in tongues. I said to myself, what is this man talking about? I said to myself, you have to receive the Holy Ghost before you speak in tongues. He, the Apostle, just kept saying speak in tongues. Then he, with hands on my head, started speaking in tongues. Then he said receive the Holy Ghost, speak in tongues. Then he started speaking in tongues. Then he said speak in tongues with his hands on my head. Then to my amazement he began to give up on me and remove his hands, I stood up so his hands could not be removed. I thought to myself, no, no, you are not going to give up on me this quick. So he let his hands stay on my head and began to speak in tongues. Then he said speak in tongues. I by this time, with the Apostle's hands on my head, was standing in front of the church facing the pews, but I did not know it. He said again speak in tongues. I said to myself this is not working, I am going to get out of here. I said to myself, the next time that he speaks in tongues I am just going to mimic him and pretend that I have the Holy Ghost so I can leave. He then spoke in tongues. Then I went to mimic him. The next thing I knew, I was speaking in a language that sounded like Hebrew, before the audience of people in the Church, motioning my hands like I was before them teaching them something. Then

I said to myself, what in the world am I doing. This was totally unlike me. Then the Apostle said, you have been filled with the Holy Ghost. Then all of a sudden I stop speaking this Hebrew like language. The Apostle just kept saying you have been filled with the Holy Ghost. I was saying to myself, is this what it is to be filled with the Holy Ghost? I did not know what to say. I did not know what to think. I went and sat back down in the same place that I was sitting before. By this time, it was time for the taping of the radio broadcast. As I sat there, Satan began to talk to me. He told me that I did not have the Holy Ghost. He said that as evil as I had been, that God would not give me the Holy Ghost. Satan then brought up to me every evil thing that I had done. He kept saying, you do not have the Holy Ghost. This went on for about an hour as I sat there. After the taping was over and I left the Church, Satan kept up his accusations and saying that I did not have the Holy Ghost. All the way as I drove home, he kept it up. When I entered into my house I said to God that if I received the Holy Ghost, let me know without a shadow of doubt. Immediately I began to speak in tongues. I was speaking loud in tongues. I began to analyze this speaking. I was not trying to mimic. My mouth and tongue were moving and I was not trying to make them move. I was speaking sounding eloquently, whatever I was speaking. This speaking went on for about an hour with me analyzing to see whether it was me or God speaking. I then thought that I might not be able to stop speaking in tongues. Immediately I stop speaking in tongues and God spoke to me clearly and said that my name had been written in the Book of Life and everything has been worth it. I knew what God meant by worth it and I started crying. All of these months. All of these weeks. All of these days. All of the praying. All of the crying. All of this seeking for the Holy Ghost, but it is worth it. Later on I would get baptized by the Apostle in the name of Jesus Christ for the remission of my sins.

This one thing I want to point out. I could have received the Holy Ghost, all the way back in October of 1985, if I had got rid of that dope and the other things of sin. You cannot hold on to the past, anything of the past that is sin, and receive the Holy Ghost. Satan would have caused me to go to hell over (2) two marijuana joints. Two joints would have kept me from immortality.

PROPHETESS SYLVIA FRANKLIN'S TESTIMONIES OF RECEIVING THE HOLY GHOST

When my wife, Prophetess Sylvia Franklin, was a child she had a very depressing life. There was constant arguing and fighting between her father and mother. Her father would be drunk and pull out a gun and threaten to kill her mother and even at certain times to kill her and her brother.

At (10) ten years old, Sylvia would look out of her window and look up and ask God to take away the gloom and let the sun shine. She always would do this. It always seemed to be so gloomy in those days. As time went by in this constant state of family turmoil, at (13) thirteen years old, God did let the sun shine in Sylvia's life. After Sylvia, her mother and brother started attending a small Holiness Church, Sylvia was involved with a street meeting service. This was Apostle William Tumlin's Church. During the meeting the people were singing and praising the Lord. Sylvia then started singing and praising the Lord and all of a sudden she started speaking in tongues.

Not really understanding what had happened to her, Sylvia was in and out of Church. As time passed Sylvia lost the Holy Ghost. At (17) seventeen years old Sylvia was in a service at Apostle William A. Tumlin's Church, All Nations Church of God. While singing and praising was taking place in the Church, Apostle Tumlin came to where Sylvia was and laid hands on her head and she started speaking in tongues. She was restored in the Holy Ghost. Later on she got baptized by Apostle Tumlin in the name of Jesus Christ for the remission of sins. Sylvia's life was never the same again.

WE DEDICATE THIS/THESE PAGE(S) OF THE BOOK IN RECOGNITION OF AND PRAISE TO JESUS FOR OUR OLDEST CHILD'S BORN AGAIN EXPERIENCE.

On January 31, 1995 our son, Elijah Jeremiah Ezekiel Franklin, had his fifth birthday. This is the same child the doctors said would have only a ten percent or less chance of being born. This is the same child some would have recommended being aborted (murdered in the womb). This is the same child who is in very good health. This is the same child the doctors said would have probable extreme health problems. This is the same child who was born premature.

After turning five years old, two days later on February 2, 1995, while we (Frederick and Sylvia) were praying for him in our house during our weekly Thursday night prayer service, he was filled with the Holy Ghost. He spoke in tongues for about an hour. After he finished speaking in tongues, we baptized him in the name of Jesus.

Through the testimony of Elijah's salvation, other children have desired to be saved and were indeed filled with the Holy Ghost and baptized in the name of Jesus.

<u>NOTE THIS</u>. Two Days After Elijah Spoke In Tongues, He Prophesied And Said, God Is Saying To Him, That We Would Be Moving To A Farm In Mobile, With Farm Animals. Later On That Year, In October, We Moved To That Farm.

THESE PAGES WE DEDICATE TO BOTH OUR SECOND SON, DANIEL ISAIAH FRANKLIN AND TO OUR YOUNGEST CHILD AND DAUGHTER, REBEKAH ANNA FRANKLIN.

This dedication is to give praise and glory to God Almighty, Father Jesus our Lord and Savior and to his Son Jesus Christ of whom the Father dwelled in on this earth, for the born again experience of Daniel Isaiah and Rebekah Anna.

June 15, 1998 was a special day in our family. This is the day that we completed household salvation in our family, the day that we could say that all five of us were born again. On this day, June 15, 1998, as we all prayed fervently during our daily dedicated afternoon prayer, God moved mightily in our presence. We were already excited for the young woman that we had prayed to receive the Holy Ghost the past night which we were preparing to baptize after our prayer time.

As we prayed fervently for God to move in a special

way that day for the souls to be saved in our community, God spoke to us to pray for Daniel and Rebekah. We, Frederick, Sylvia and Elijah, started praying for them to be filled with the Holy Ghost. As we prayed, we noticed that Daniel and Rebekah were under the influence of the presence of God in praising him and they began to speak in tongues. We wondered could this actually be happening this fast as we had been praying for? Could our five year old son and four year old daughter now finally be filled with the Holy Ghost? We had been praying to God every day since they were conceived in Sylvia's womb for them to receive the Holy Ghost. We didn't really know whether they were speaking in tongues or not at this time because during prayer our children often would mimic us when we were speaking in tongues. But, this time seemed to be different, especially with Rebekah. Daniel Isaiah, every since he was about one year old, always has fervently praised the Lord, singing, dancing, lifting up his hands to God and appearing to speak in tongues. Rebekah, however, did not normally praise God as enthusiastically as did Daniel. But on this day, June 15, 1998, at about 2:00 p.m., our little Rebekah was on fire! And even the normally enthusiastic Daniel seemed to have a double portion. We looked at them and wondered could this actually be it? Could our Daniel Isaiah be filled with the Holy Ghost? Could our son, who was born three months premature, be now born again of the Spirit? Could our son, who at one time only weighed (2) two pounds and (13) thirteen ounces, be born again of the Spirit? Could our son, who the doctors said would have to stay in the hospital for at least three months after he was born, who only stayed one month because he was so healthy, could he actually be speaking in tongues? Could this, our son who is strong and in excellent health who doctors said would have severe and numerous health problems, be born again of the Spirit? Could it also be that our little Rebekah be born again of the Spirit? Could it be that the Daddy's little girl, that he calls "Pretty Pretty" be born again of the Spirit? Could both Daniel Isaiah and Rebekah be filled with the Holy Ghost? Could Frederick now release our second book for publication after waiting for Daniel and Rebekah to be born again so he could dedicate some pages in the book to their born again experience as he had done in our first with Elijah?

We did not want to make a mistake here and tell Daniel and Rebekah that they had been filled with the Holy Ghost, it was too important. We had to be sure. So, we prayed to God for him to tell us clearly whether they had been filled with the Holy Ghost or not.

God answered us quickly and said yes. We were exceedingly glad and satisfied. But, to our shame and astonishment, God also said that Daniel had been filled with the Holy Ghost before now. God did not tell us when, neither did we know. We suspected it was during one of our weekly Thursday night prayer services or during one of our three daily prayer times. God would later let us know that Daniel had received the Holy Ghost when he was (3) three years old during one of our weekly night services. Although we were shamed and rightly so, for not knowing our son was already filled with the Holy Ghost, our joy was rekindled and we went immediately and baptized Daniel Isaiah and Rebekah Anna in the name of Jesus for the remission of their sins to complete their born again experience.

REASONS TO WANT
TO BE SAVED

Why would you want to be saved? Well, I will give you three good reasons to want to be saved. You might say, I don't need to be saved. You might say, I'm doing just fine like I am. Well, you might have an argument if you could guarantee the future would be what you want it to be. You might have an argument if you could guarantee that you will be living next year. You might have an argument if you could guarantee that you will be living next month. You might have an argument if you could guarantee that you will be living next week. You might have an argument if you could guarantee that you will be living tomorrow. You might have an argument if you could guarantee you will not die today. You might have an argument if you could guarantee that you will not die the next hour. You might have an argument if you can ensure that you will be living the next five minutes. If you had control over your time of life, you might not need Jesus' salvation. But, since Jesus, the God Almighty, has control over your appointed time of life, if you are not totally stupid, then you should realize that you need to be saved.

This is the bottom line, either ignorance or stupidity causes you not to get saved. Jesus, the God Almighty, before the world was created, assigned an appointed time for each of us to be born. He, also, set the exact time of our death. Jesus has assigned us our parking meter of life. Who is familiar with a prepaid cell phone? Well, for a prepaid cell phone, you have an allotted amount of minutes to use your cell phone. Once you have used all of your minutes, it is useless. It is dead. Well, Jesus, the God Almighty, has assigned us our prepaid cell phone of life. Do you know how many minutes you have left? Supposed you have (15) fifteen minutes left. Suppose (10) ten. Suppose (5) five. Do you know whether an earthquake will now occur at this place or not? Do you know whether an airplane will now or not crash into this building? Do you know whether a terrorist will now or not blow up this building? Jesus knows. Do you know whether you will or will not fall dead in this minute of a heart attack? Do you know on the way from here whether you will have an head on collision with another vehicle and be killed? Jesus knows. Your time clock of life is running out!

The number one trick of Satan is to convince those that are not saved, who want to be saved, that you have more time, until your parking meter of life expires. He hopes to convince you that you have more time, until your prepaid cell phone of life is used up.

You might be one of the fools that might say, that you do not care whether you die without being saved. If this is you, you are indeed a fool. One of the main reasons to get saved is to stay out of hell. If you are one of the ones that say you do not care whether you die without being saved, then you probably do not understand that there is a hell with a wide opened mouth waiting to swallow you. Hell is a real place. When death occurs, you, the real you, your soul, will either go to hell or heaven. If you are saved, you go to heaven. If you are not saved, you go to hell. What is hell, you might ask? Hell is a place where souls are tormented with fire. A very, very, very, hot fire. The hottest fire that we can make on earth, spirits can touch it, walk in, lay on, etc., without it burning them. Spirits are beings that include angels and devils. God, also, is a spirit. Hell is so hot that it burns spirits. Not God, but other Spirits. A person's soul is spirit. A person's soul is the person's desire, feeling, emotions, mind, hearing, sight, taste, smell and memory. The real person. The real you. The body dies and rots. The soul is eternal. It will live either in hell or with God, forever and ever more. Hell is a place located in the center of the earth. Those that are in hell are in continual torment. They are burning continually. There is no relief. Just continual screaming and burning. No rest day nor night. There is no water. There is no air conditioner. There is no fan. There is no kind of cooling. Remember, understand, that they have their feelings in hell. Remember, understand, that they have their desires in hell. Their desire to quench their thirst can never be satisfied. Their desire to alter their circumstances can never be done. Their desire to leave hell will never be fulfilled. They will be in their forever. Their cry out to God for help will be in vain. Hopelessness! Hopelessness! Hopelessness! Pain of burning continually. The pain from a burning fire, if not the worst, is one of the worse pains that you can have. Pains on your hands. Pains on your feet. Pains on your arms. Pains on your legs. Pains on your back. Pains on your belly. Pains on your chest. Pains on your face. Pains on your ears. Pains on your tongue. Pains on the top of your head. Pain everywhere. Pains all the time. All day and all night forever and ever and ever and ever and evermore. They had an alternative, they had another choice, they could have gotten saved.

This is the second good reason to want to get saved. For those of you that believe that there is a God, then you should want to be saved for your love to God. You know that God is a good God, the good

God. You know that God has been good to you. You cannot live without God. You cannot walk without God. You cannot talk without God. You cannot eat without God. You cannot sleep without God. You cannot love without God. You cannot be loved without God. You cannot breathe without God. All of these things and many, many, other good things God provides you. And, not only you, but all others even his enemies. Even those that curse him. Even those who prefer to serve Satan rather than God himself. It was God who protected you from death. It was Satan who tried to kill you. It was God who healed you. It was Satan that made you sick. It was Satan who killed your love ones. It was God who protected your love ones from Satan that allowed them to live as long as they did.

To get saved is to show your love and gratitude to God. To get saved is to show your love and gratitude to God for a price that he paid for your salvation. The price was very great. God allowed his Son Jesus of Nazareth to die. There have been some men who have allowed their sons to die for what they considered a good cause or for a friend. God allowed his son to die for his enemies. God, even, allowed his Son to suffer for his enemies. To suffer such suffering never suffered before. Unbearable sufferings. God allowed him to be slapped. God allowed him to be spit on. God allowed his beard to be pulled off of his face, causing pain and bleeding and swelling. God allowed a crown made of thorns to be put on his head. Shoved into his scalp and forehead, causing pain, bleeding and swelling. God allowed his Son to be beat with (39) thirty-nine strokes of a whip that would snatch the meat off his bones. Pain, excruciating pain, bleeding and swelling. God allowed him to be nailed on a tree in his hands and feet, causing pain, excruciating pain, bleeding and swelling. God saw his son suffer. He saw his body bleed, from the top of his head to the bottom of his feet. God saw his Son's body swell, from the top of his head to the bottom of his feet. God saw his Son's body from the top of his head to the bottom of his feet change to a painful black and blue-like color with pain and red with blood. He saw him agonize in pain and misery, until through the bleeding and swelling he was not recognizable as a man. We would not and could not allow our sons and daughters, who we loved, to suffer even for a friend, let along their enemies. All that God has done for us, so much, and He only requires for a token of love, for us to accept his glorious salvation. For us to stay out of hell. So, for those who believe that there is a God, God Almighty, then our love for God should make us want to be saved. To get saved is to show that God's sacrifice of His Son was not in vain with us. This salvation of ours makes God's investment yield a return. So great investment for such a little return. Without your salvation the little return is even smaller. Just think, by getting saved, the God that created the universe will allow us to be with him for ever and ever more. It will not be just any existence, but God has promised us in the Holy Bible, that we will have no more sorrow, no more pain, no more crying and no more death. I believe that God has allowed me to experience how it will be in heaven. Not long after I was filled with the Holy Ghost, while living in Montgomery, Alabama, God gave me a visitation. While sitting in my bed, with my legs and my feet in the bed, eyes wide opened, the presence, the glory, the anointing of God, moved on me. I felt it. I knew somehow it was God. I don't know how I knew, but I knew without a shadow of doubt that it was God. The sensation, the feeling, started at the bottom of my feet. It then covered my feet. It proceeded up my legs. It continued up my body. It covered my thighs. It just continued to go up my body. It covered my belly and chest. Then it went in my shoulders and through my arms, hands and fingers. It went up my neck and covered my head. It was all over me. Let me try to tell you how it felt. Words cannot properly explain how good it felt. This felt at least a hundred times better than the best feeling I have ever had. There is nothing we have experience to compare with it. Let me tell you this. Everything on me felt good. My fingernails, even, felt good. My hair, even, felt good. Even each strand of hair felt good. It felt so good until I started asking God to allow those that I knew to experience it. I started calling out their names for God to allow them to feel it. I mentioned my mother, brother, sisters, grandmother, nieces, nephews, aunts, uncles, first cousins, second cousins, other relatives, friends, co-workers, college classmates that were friends, church members and maybe some others, for God to allow to experience what I was feeling. I don't know the exact time, this feeling, this presence, this anointing, this visitation, lasted. It was a long time. Maybe an hour or longer. I believe God allowed me to experience what heaven feels like. People, if this is what heaven feels like, this along is worth getting saved for.

Now I will address the third good reason to get saved. If you are one who thinks that to be saved has no present life benefit, consider this. Soon in these days, there will be a great tormenting plague to cover the whole earth. This will happen very soon. Possibly, during George W. Bush's time as President. This torment will be excruciating pain. This pain will be continual. It will affect all ages, babies, young children, teenagers, young adults, middle age adults, senior citizens, all. The pain of this plague will be so horrible, until the people will want to die. People will want to commit suicide. There will be no medicine for cure. There will be no medicine for relief. There will be screaming all over the earth. The children will be screaming. The parents will be screaming. The grandparents will be screaming. The great grandparents will be screaming. The nurses will be screaming. The doctors will be screaming. Those of the police force will be screaming. Those of the army will be screaming. Those of the Air Force will be screaming. Those of the Navy will be screaming. Those of the Marines will be screaming. The members of the House of Representatives will be screaming. The Senators will be screaming. The Supreme Court Justices will be screaming. The Vice President will be screaming. The President will be screaming. The Pope will scream. All will scream!

All of this paining. All of this misery. All of this hurting and no relief. No relief for five months. Yes! It will last for (5) five months. And think about this. It is hard to get sleep when you are in pain. What hopelessness. The curse of this plague will be so bad that people will want to die. However, the curse of this plague will not allow them to die. This curse has been told about in the Book of Revelation of the Holy Bible. Turn to the Book of Revelation in your Bible. Look at Chapter (9) Nine. Read Verse (6) Six.

<u>Revelation Ch.9, V.6</u>

"And in those days shall men seek death, and shall not find it; and shall desire to die and death shall flee from them."

This great excruciating painful plague will soon happen. This painful plague will be the closest thing to hell itself. It will be so horrible, so excruciating, that God told me to write a book about it to warn the people. This is the book here. The name is "Five Month Desire To Die, But Not Possible When Fifth Angel Blows Trumpet." The only ones on planet Earth that will not be affected with this great painful plague, will be those that have the Holy Ghost. You must have the Holy Ghost to be saved. All that have the Holy Ghost speak in tongues.

If you, yet, after reading this, due to some custom, tradition or religion, do not get saved, it is because you are too stupid to get saved.

<u>THE FOUR EASY STEPS TO GET SAVED/BORN AGAIN:</u>

1. Repent:
   a. ask God to forgive your sins, ask in the name of Jesus;
   b. surrender your will for God's will to be done in your life.
2. Ask God to save you, to fill you with the Holy Ghost, ask in the name of Jesus.

3. Do not ask God anymore to save you, just thank God, praise God for saving you. You must thank God in the name of Jesus. At the point of your greatest sincerity, you will speak in another language. This will be your sign of confirmation. God will be using your mouth to speak a language spoken somewhere on earth that you have not learned. This is your sign that you are born of the Spirit.
4. Get baptized in the name of Jesus Christ.

John Ch.3,Vs.3&5
"Jesus answered...Except a man be born again, he cannot see the kingdom of God...Jesus answered... Except a man be born of water and of the Spirit he cannot enter into the kingdom of God."

John Ch.3,V.8
"...thou hearest the sound thereof...so is everyone that is born of the Spirit."

Colossians Ch.3,V.17
"And whatsoever ye do in word or deed, do all in the name of the Lord Jesus..."

LIST OF BOOKS THAT
WE HAVE WRITTEN:

1. Proof That **YOUR LEADERS** Have **DECEIVED YOU** And The End Times

2. What **GOD** Is Now Telling His Prophets **ABOUT** The **END TIMES**

3. Five Month **DESIRE TO DIE**, But Not Possible When Fifth Angel Blows Trumpet

4. **GOD's** Word Concern **MARRIAGE AND DIVORCE**

5. The Name Of The (Anti-Christ) Beast And **666** Identification

6. **WHERE GOD's PEOPLE** (Saints) **GO** When GOD Comes Back To Get Us

7. How You Can **PROVE** That **YOU HAVE** A **SOUL**

8. **JESUS** Was **NOT CRUCIFIED WHEN** As Has Been **TAUGHT**

9. Reasons For **JEWS** To Believe That **JESUS** Is The **MESSIAH**

10. **THE** Big **LIE**

11. Proof: The **TRINITY** Doctrine **IS A LIE**

24. **MAKING SATAN** And His Kingdom **PAY** A Big Price **SO** The **END CAN COME**

25. Makeup, Membership And Money Of **GOD'S CHURCH** And **HOW GOD WANTS** Them To Be

26. Events Of The **SEVEN SEALS** And The **COINCIDING** End Time **EVENTS** Mentioned Elsewhere In The Bible

27. **WHEN** The **END** Will **COME**

28. The **JUDGMENT OF** The **UNITED STATES**

29. What **GOD** Has Shown And Said **TO** And Concerning **THE FRANKLIN'S** Family

30. How Any Candidate Can **GET** The **VOTE FROM** GOD'S **PEOPLE**, Denominations And Catholics

31. The **LOST REVELATION**

32. **NEW YORK CITY** Becomes The **CAPITAL** Of The **NEW WORLD ORDER**

33. A Man Named **BUSH PREPARES** The **WAY FOR** The **ANTI-CHRIST**

34. **MARCH** Was When **JESUS** Was **BORN** And **NOT CHRISTMAS**

35. **GOD'S FOUR** Healings And Deliverances Which He **DESIRES FOR US**

HOW TO GET SAVED

To Be Saved You must Speak with Tongues & Be Baptized in the Name of Jesus

John Ch. 3, V. 3
"Jesus answered... Except a man be born again, he cannot see the Kingdom of God."

John Ch. 3, V. 5
"Jesus answered... Except a man be born of water and of the Spirit, he cannot enter into the Kingdom of God."

Acts Ch. 2, V. 38
"... Repent, and be baptized every one of you in the name of Jesus Christ for the remission of sins, and ye shall receive the gift of the Holy Ghost."

How to Repent: (1) Sincerely ask God to forgive your sins, ask in the name of Jesus; (2) Surrender your will for God's Will to be done in your life.

After Repenting: Sincerely ask God to save you, to give you his Spirit, to give you the Holy Ghost, to have you to speak with other tongues. [Once you have asked, then just continue to thank God for doing so, just praise him, sincerely. You WILL then speak in tongues.]

John Ch. 3, V. 8
"... thou hearest the sound thereof...so is everyone that is born of the Spirit."

After Speaking in Tongues: Get baptized in the name of Jesus, again you must be repented.

NOTE: You can be baptized and then receive the Holy Ghost or be filled with the Holy Ghost then be baptized.

Speaking in Tongues: Speaking in tongues (unknown language) is God speaking through you.

Mark Ch. 16, V. 17
"And these signs shall follow them that believe... they shall speak with new tongues."

Acts Ch. 2, V. 4
"... and began to speak with other tongues as the Spirit gave them utterance."

Acts Ch. 22, V 16
"... be baptized, and wash away thy sins..."

Colossians Ch. 3, V. 17
"And whatsoever ye do in word or deed, do all in the name of the Lord Jesus..."

The name of the Father is Jesus, the name of the Son is Jesus, the name of the Holy Ghost is Jesus.

John Ch. 17, V. 26
"And I have declared thy name unto them..."

John Ch. 5, V. 43 "
"I am come in my Father's name..."

Hebrews Ch. 1, V. 4
"... he hath by inheritance obtained a more excellent name..."

John Ch. 4, V. 24
"God is a Spirit..."

Question: Is the Father Holy? Answer: Yes. God is a Father; God was manifested in flesh as a Son; God is a Spirit, the Holy Spirit, the Holy Ghost.

I, Frederick E. Franklin, am a Father, am a Son, am a Human Being. Father, Son, Holy Ghost and Father, Son, Human Being are titles. God's name is Jesus.

Matthew Ch. 28, V. 19
"... Teach all nations, baptizing them in the name of ... the Son..."

TO BE A PART OF THE F&SF MINISTRY FOR JESUS THE FOLLOWING WILL BE EXPECTED:

II Timothy Ch.2, V.3

"Thou therefore endure hardness, as a good soldier of Jesus Christ."

Ephesians Ch.6, V.10

"... be strong in the Lord, and in the power of his might."

Ephesians Ch.5, V.27

"That he might present it to himself a glorious church, not having spot, or wrinkle, or any such thing; but that it should be holy and without blemish."

The F&SF Ministry For JESUS Soldier Will:

1. Be Filled With The Holy Ghost (Evidenced By Speaking In Tongues)

2. Be Baptized In The Name Of JESUS

3. Be Honest And Sincere

4. Have Love And Compassion For Others

5. Properly Pay Tithes And Give Offerings

6. Believe In One God (The God Of Abraham, Isaac, And Jacob)

7. Worship Only God Almighty, The Creator Of The Universe, JESUS

8. Be Holy

9. Attend Sabbath (Friday Dark To Saturday Dark) Service(s)

10. Attend Other Service(s) When Possible

11. Make Continuous Sincere Efforts For Souls To Be Saved

12. Profess/Testify That You Must Speak In Tongues And Be Baptized In The Name Of Jesus To Be Saved

13. Profess/Testify That The Great Tribulation Is Before The Rapture

14. Reveal That Pope John Paul II Is The (Anti-Christ) Beast

15. Be Bold (Not A Coward)

16. Desire To Grow In Revelation And Power Of God

17. Be Faithful And Dedicated To The F&SF Ministry For JESUS

18. Receive/Accept The Teachings Of Apostle Frederick E. Franklin

19. Not Espouse Teachings/Doctrines Contrary To That Of Apostle Frederick E. Franklin

20. Adhere To The Leadership Of Apostle Frederick E. Franklin

21. Not Be A Liar

22. Not Be A Hypocrite

23. Not Be A Witchcraft Worker

24. Not Be A Partaker Of Idolatry.

EXCERPTS FROM OUR BOOK "THE NAME OF THE (ANTI-CHRIST) BEAST AND 666 IDENTIFICATION"

There will be great deception. The scriptures indicate that the (Anti-Christ) Beast, Pope John Paul II, Carol Josef Wojtyla, will fake his death. Later on, to fake being resurrected from the dead. All to the end, to fake that he is God. All to the end, to discredit JESUS' resurrection. All to the end, to discredit that JESUS is God and rather to show/deceive that he is God.

Revelation Ch. 17, V. 8
"...the beast that was, and is not, and yet is."

The Above scripture indicates that the Beast, Pope John Paul II, Carol Josef Wojtyla, was living. It further indicates that he will seem not to be living, but he actually will be living. He was living. He appears not to be living. But, he yet is living.

(PURCHASE OUR BOOKS)

BY FREDERICK E. FRANKLIN

BOOKSTORE SALES:
(25,000 BOOKSTORES)

1. BARNES & NOBLE
2. BOOKS A MILLION
3. ETC.

INTERNET SALES:
AMAZON . COM

DIRECT SALES:
2669 MEADOWVIEW DR.
MOBILE, ALABAMA 36695
PH. # : (251) 644-4329

JESUS IS GOD

1. <u>I John Chapter 5, Verse 20</u>
"And we know that the Son of God is come, and hath given us an understanding, that we may know him that is true, and we are in him that is true, even in his Son Jesus Christ. This is the true God, and eternal life."

2. <u>John Chapter 1, Verses 1 & 14</u>
"In the beginning was the Word, and the Word was with God, and the Word was God. And the Word was made flesh, and dwelt among us, (and we beheld his glory, the glory as of the only begotten of the Father,) full of grace and truth."

3. <u>I Timothy Chapter 3, Verse 16</u>
"And without controversy great is the mystery of godliness: God was manifest in the flesh, justified in the Spirit, seen of angels, preached unto the Gentiles, believed on in the world, received up into glory."

4. <u>Isaiah Chapter 9, Verse 6</u>
"For unto us a child is born, unto us a son is given: and the government shall be upon his shoulder: and his name shall be called Wonderful, Counsellor,

The mighty God, The everlasting Father, The Prince of Peace."

5. <u>Matthew Chapter 1, Verse 23</u>
"Behold, a virgin shall be with child, and shall bring forth a son, and they shall call his name Emmanuel, which being interpreted is, God with us."

6. <u>Titus Chapter 1, Verses 3 & 4</u>
"...God our Saviour;...the Lord Jesus Christ our Saviour."

7. <u>Isaiah Chapter 43, Verse 11</u>
"I, even I, am the Lord; and beside me there is no Saviour."

8. <u>Isaiah Chapter 44, Verse 6</u>
"Thus saith the Lord the King of Israel, and his redeemer the Lord of hosts; I am the first, and I am the last; and beside me there is no God."

9. <u>Revelation Chapter 1, Verses 17 & 18</u>
"...I am the first and the last: I am he that liveth, and was dead..."

10. <u>Revelation Chapter 22, Verses 13 & 16</u>
"I am Alpha and Omega, the beginning and the end, the first and the last. I Jesus have sent mine angel to testify unto you these things in the churches..."

11. <u>Isaiah Chapter 44, Verse 24</u>
"Thus saith the Lord, thy redeemer, and he that formed thee from the womb, I am the Lord that maketh all things; that stretcheth forth the heavens alone; that spreadeth abroad the earth by myself..."

12. <u>Colossians Chapter 1, Verses 16, 17 & 18</u>
"For by him were all things created, that are in heaven, and that are in earth, visible and invisible, whether they be thrones, or powers: all things were created by him, and for him: And he is before all things, and by him all things consist. And he is the head of the body the church."

13. <u>Ephesians Chapter 5, Verse 23</u>
"For the husband is the head of the wife, even as Christ is the head of the church: and he is the saviour of the body."

14. <u>Colossians Chapter 2, Verse 9</u>
"For in Him dwelleth all the fullness of the Godhead bodily."

15. <u>I John Chapter 5, Verse 7</u>
"...three that bear record in heaven, the Father, the Word, and the Holy Ghost: and these three are one."

16. <u>Revelation Chapter 15, Verse 3</u>
"...Great and Marvelous are thy works, Lord God Almighty; just and true are thy ways, thou King of saints."

17. <u>Revelation Chapter 17, Verse 14</u>
"...and the Lamb shall overcome them: for he is Lord of lords, and King of kings; and they that are with him are called, and chosen, and faithful."

18. <u>I Thessalonians Chapter 3, Verse 13</u>
"...God, even our Father, at the coming of our Lord Jesus Christ with all his saints."

19. <u>Zechariah Chapter 14, Verse 5</u>
"...and the Lord my God shall come, and all the saints with thee."

20. <u>I John Chapter 3, Verse 16</u>
"Hereby perceive we the love of God, because he laid down his life for us."

21. Etc.

<u>THE FOUR EASY STEPS TO GET SAVED/BORN AGAIN</u>:
1. Repent:
    a. ask God to forgive your sins, ask in the name of Jesus;
    b. surrender your will for God's will to be done in your life.

2. Ask God to save you, to fill you with the Holy Ghost, ask in the name of Jesus.

3. Do not ask God anymore to save you, just thank God, praise God for saving you. You must thank God in the name of Jesus. At the point of your greatest sincerity, you will speak in another language. This will be your sign of confirmation. God will be using your mouth to speak a language spoken somewhere on earth that you have not learned. This is your sign that you are born of the Spirit.

4. Get baptized in the name of Jesus Christ.

John Ch.3,Vs.3&5

"Jesus answered...Except a man be born again, he cannot see the kingdom of God...Jesus answered... Except a man be born of water and of the Spirit he cannot enter into the kingdom of God."

John Ch.3,V.8

"...thou hearest the sound thereof...so is everyone that is born of the Spirit."

Colossians Ch.3,V.17

"And whatsoever ye do in word or deed, do all in the name of the Lord Jesus..."

THE SABBATH

What Is The Sabbath?
The Sabbath is a holy day ordained by God to be so. It is a day for all to cease from work.

When Is The Sabbath?
The Sabbath is the last day, the seventh day of the week.

<u>Genesis Ch.2, Vs. 1-3</u>
"Thus the heavens and earth were finished, and all of the host of them. And on the seventh day God ended his work which he had made; and he rested on the seventh day from all his work which he had made."

<u>Exodus Ch.20, Vs. 8-11</u>
"Remember the sabbath day, to keep it holy. Six days shalt thou labour, and do all thy work: But the seventh day is the sabbath of the Lord thy God: in it thou shalt not do any work, thou, nor thy son, nor thy daughter, thy manservant, nor thy cattle, nor thy stranger that is within thy gates: For in six days the Lord made heaven and earth, the sea, and all that in them is, and rested the seventh day:

wherefore the Lord blessed the sabbath day, and hallowed it."

Exodus Ch.23, V. 12
"Six days thou shalt do thy work, and on the seventh day thou shalt rest: that thine ox and thine ass may rest, and the son of thy handmaid, and the stranger, may be refreshed."

When Does The Day Start?
The day starts at dark and goes to the next day at dark.

Genesis Ch.1, Vs 5, 8, 13, 19, 23 & 31
"...And the evening and the morning were the first day...And the evening and the morning were the second day. And the evening and the morning were the third day. And the evening and the morning were the fourth day. And the evening and the morning were the fifth day. And God saw every thing that he had made and, behold, it was very good. And the evening and the morning were the sixth day."

Is It A Sin To NOT Keep Or Violate The Sabbath?
To keep the Sabbath is one of the ten commandments. One of the ten commandments say thou shalt not kill. Another says thou shalt not steal. Just as it is sin to kill and steal, likewise, is it a sin to NOT keep or to violate the Sabbath.

Exodus Ch.20, V. 13-15

"Thou shalt not kill. Thou shalt not commit adultery. Thou shalt not steal."

What You Should Not Do On The Sabbath.

Exodus Ch.20, V. 10

"But the seventh day is the sabbath of the Lord thy God: in it thou shalt not do any work, thou, nor thy son, nor thy daughter, thy manservant, nor thy maidservant, nor thy cattle, nor thy stranger that is within thy gates..."

Nehemiah Ch.10, V. 31

"And if the people of the land bring ware or any victuals on the sabbath day to sell, that we would not buy it of them on the sabbath, or on the holy day..."

Nehemiah Ch.13, Vs. 16-18

"There dwelt men of Tyre also therein, which brought fish, and all manner of ware, and sold on the sabbath unto the children of Judah, and in Jerusalem. Then I contended with nobles of Judah, and said unto them, What evil thing is this that ye do, and profane the sabbath day? Did not your fathers thus, and did not our God bring all this wrath upon this city? Yet ye bring more wrath upon Israel by profaning the sabbath."

What Happened When The Sabbath Was Not Kept Or Violated Intentionally.

Numbers Ch.15, Vs. 32-36

"And while the children of Israel were in the wilderness, they found a man that gathered sticks upon the sabbath day. And they that found him gathering sticks brought him unto Moses and Aaron and unto all the congregation. And they put him in ward, because it was not declared what should be done unto him. And the Lord said unto Moses, The man shall be surely put to death: all the congregation shall stone him with stones without the camp. And all the congregation brought him without the camp, and stone with stones and he died; as the Lord commanded Moses."

Numbers Ch.15, Vs. 30-31

"But the soul that doeth ought presumptuously, whether he be born in the land, or a stranger, the same reproacheth the Lord; and that soul shall be cut off from among his people. Because he hath despised the word of the Lord, and hath broken his commandment, that soul shall be utterly cut off; his iniquity shall be upon."

Not Keeping Or Violating The Sabbath Out Of Ignorance.

Numbers Ch.15, Vs. 27-28
"And if any soul sin through ignorance...the priest shall make atonement for the soul that sinneth ignorantly, when he sinneth by ignorance before the Lord, to make atonement for him; and it shall be forgiven him."

Numbers Ch.15, Vs. 22, 24-25
"And if ye erred, and not observed at all these commandments...Then if it shall be, if ought be committed by ignorance without the knowledge... the priest shall make an atonement for all the congregation of the children of Israel, and it shall be forgiven them..."

Other Benefits Of Keeping The Sabbath.
God is pleased with those who obey his word and the promises of the Holy Bible is available to you.

Isaiah Ch.56 Vs. 2, 5-7
"Blessed is the man that doeth this, and the son of man that layeth hold on it; that keepeth the sabbath from polluting it, and keep his hand from doing any evil. Even unto them will I give in mine house and within my walls a place and a name better than the sons and daughters. I will give them an everlasting name, that shall not be cut off. Also the sons of the

stranger that join themselves to the Lord, to serve him, and to love the name of the Lord, to be his servants, every one that keepeth the sabbath from polluting it, and taketh hold of my covenant; Even them will I bring unto my holy mountain, and make them joyful in my house of prayer...their sacrifices shall be accepted upon mine altar; for mine house shall be called an house of prayer for all people."

Exodus Ch.23, V. 12
"...thou shalt rest...be refreshed."

Exodus Ch.20, V.12
"...the Lord blessed the sabbath day, and hallowed it."

Why Has Sunday Been Chosen As The So-Called Sabbath By The So-Called Christians And Some Christians?

The Pope of 325 A.D. birth this blasphemy of changing the Sabbath day from the seventh day to the first day of the week. This blasphemous change of the sabbath to Sunday was done to have the people worship God the Almighty on the same day as the worship of the sun god. Sunday the worship of the Sun god. This blasphemous change was prophesied of in the scriptures.

Matthew Ch.24, V. 24
"For there shall arise false Christs, and false prophets, and shall shew great signs and wonders; insomuch that, if it were possible, they shall deceive the very elect."

Daniel Ch.7, V. 25
"And he shall speak great words against the most High, and shall wear out the saints of the most High, and think to change times and laws..."

Daniel Ch.8, V. 12
"An host was given him against the daily sacrifice by reason of transgression, and it cast down the truth to the ground; and it practiced and prospered."

To justify this blasphemous change, he, the Pope, had to use scriptures of the Holy Bible. He used three places in the scriptures.

Matthew Ch.28, Vs. 1-6
"In the end of the sabbath, as it began to dawn toward the first day of the week, came Mary Magdalene and the other Mary to see the sepulchre. And, behold, there was a great earthquake: for the angel of Lord descended from heaven, and came and rolled back the stone from the door, and sat upon it. His countenance was like lightning, and his raiment white as snow; And for fear of him the keepers did shake, and became as dead men. And

the angel answered and said unto the women, Fear ye not: for I know that ye seek Jesus, which was crucified. He is not here: for he is risen, as he said. Come, see the place where the Lord lay."

Supposedly, because Jesus was resurrected on the first day of the week, the sabbath should be changed to the first day of the week.

I Corinthians Ch.16, Vs. 1-3
"Now concerning the collection for the saints, as I have given order to the churches of Galatia, even so do ye. Upon the first day of the week let every one of you lay by him in store, as God hath prospered him, that there be no gatherings when I come. And when I come, whosoever ye shall approve by your letters, them will I send to bring your liberality to Jerusalem."

Supposedly, because Paul told them to take up a collection on the first day of the week, this, therefore, means that the New Testament Church's sabbath is on the first day of the week.

Acts Ch.20, V. 7
"And upon the first day of the week, when the disciples came together to break bread, Paul preached to them, ready to depart on the morrow, and continued his speech until midnight."

Supposedly, because the disciples came together on the first day means that they came to hear the word, and because Paul preached on the first day, supposedly, this shows that the New Testament Church had as its sabbath the first day of the week.

What ridiculous justification(s) to change the Sabbath to the first day of the week.

Scriptures Of The New Testament Refuting The So-Called Sunday Sabbath.

Let us first look at the Pope's last so-called justification, Acts Ch.20, V. 7. When the scriptures said that they came "together to break bread," it means that they came together to eat. While they were there together, Paul took this opportunity to preached to them. Like any preacher would do. Refer to the immediate following scriptures, Acts Ch.20, Vs. 8-12.

Acts Ch.20, Vs. 8-12

"And there were many lights in the upper chamber, where they were gathered together. And there sat in the window a certain young man named Eutychus, being fallen into a deep sleep: and as Paul was long preaching, he sunk down with sleep, and fell down from the third loft, and was taken up dead. And Paul went down, and fell on him, and embracing him said, Trouble not yourselves; for his life is in him. When he therefore was come up again, and had broken bread, and eaten, and talked a long while, even till break of day, so he departed. And they brought the young man alive, and were not a little comforted."

Let us now look at the Pope's I Corinthians Ch.16, Vs. 1-3, justification. Here Paul tells the Church of Corinth to give an offering to the Church in Jerusalem. He said take up collection on the first day of the week. Note that Paul said that there should not be any gathering. The people could not gather on the sabbath day to sell or give their goods or livestock to get a collection, so Paul said do it on the first day of the week. And whatever they gathered on the first day of the week, that is where their offering would come from.

Let us now look at the Pope's third and remaining justification, Matthew Ch.28, Vs. 1-6. These scriptures speak of Jesus' resurrection on the first day of they week. Somehow, this gives us the right to change God's word of a seventh day Sabbath. This is nonsense. God says that there is nothing above his word, not even the name of Jesus.

Psalm 138, V. 2
"I will worship toward thy holy temple, and praise thy name for thy lovingkindness and for thy truth:

for thou hast magnified thy word above all thy name."

Now let us see when Paul, Jews and the Gentiles, the New Testament Church, really worshipped. When their Sabbath actually was.

<u>Acts Ch.18, V. 4</u>
"And he reasoned in the synagogue every Sabbath, and persuaded the Jews and the Greeks"

<u>Acts Ch.13, Vs. 13-17, 22-23, 42-44</u>
"Now when Paul and his company loosed from Paphos...they came to Antioch...and went into the synagogue on the sabbath day, and sat down. And after the reading of the law and the prophets the rulers of the synagogue sent unto them, saying, Ye men and brethren, if ye have any word of exhortation for the people, say on. Then Paul stood up, and beckoning with his hand said, Men of Israel, and ye that fear God, give audience. The God of this people of Israel chose our fathers... he raised up unto them David to be their King... Of this man's seed hath God according to his promise raised unto Israel a Savior, Jesus...And when the Jews were gone out of the synagogue, the Gentiles besought that these words might be preached to them the next sabbath. Now when the congregation was broken up, many of the Jews and

religious proselytes followed Paul...And the next sabbath day came almost the whole city together to hear the word of God."

Note: Jews that worshipped God, only worshipped on the seventh day, the real Sabbath day.

<u>I Peter Ch.3, Vs. 15-16</u>
"But sanctify the Lord God in your hearts: and be ready always to give an answer to every man that asketh you a reason of the hope that is in you with meekness and fear: Having a good conscience; that, whereas they speak evil of you, as of evildoers, they may be ashamed that falsely accuse your good conversation in Christ."

What About Colossians Chapter 2, Verse 16?

<u>Colossians Ch.2, V. 16</u>
Let no man judge you in meat, or in drink, or respect of an holyday, or of the new moon, or of the sabbaths..."

There are more than one kind of sabbath referred to in the Holy Bible. There is the seventh day sabbath as has been discussed thus far and there are other sabbaths and holydays. These other sabbaths and holydays are what is referred to in Colossians Chapter 2, Verse 16. These sabbaths included the Passover, feast days, and some other holydays observed by the Jews. Among these days was The Dedication Of The Temple built by Solomon.

<u>John Ch.10, Vs. 22-23</u>
"And it was at Jerusalem the feast of the dedication, and it was winter. And Jesus walked in the temple in Solomon's porch."

Another such sabbath day is referred to in John Chapter 19, Verse 31.

<u>John Ch.19, V. 31</u>
"The Jews therefore, because it was the preparation, that the bodies should not remain upon the cross on the sabbath day, (for that sabbath was an high day,)..."

The lack of understanding of the above scripture is how the Pope of 325 A.D. has been able to deceive the people in celebrating the worship of the Spring goddess. This is the Easter celebration. Refer to our book, "Jesus Was Not Crucified When As Has Been Taught."

Here are some of the scriptures referring to the other sabbaths: Leviticus Ch.19, Vs. 1-3; Leviticus Ch.19, V. 30; Leviticus Ch.16, Vs. 29-31; Leviticus Ch.25, Vs. 1-5; Leviticus Ch.26, Vs. 27-35; Leviticus Ch.23, Vs. 4-7; Leviticus Ch.23, Vs. 15, 21, 23-28, 32-36 & 38-39; I Kings Ch.8, Vs. 63-66; etc.

These are the ordinances that Jesus blotted out, even nailing to them the cross.

SPECIAL EXCEPTIONS TO WORKING ON THE SABBATH:

People who try to get around the word of God concerning not working on the Sabbath, try to use certain instances when JESUS said it was alright to do certain things on the Sabbath. They point to the scriptures when JESUS' disciples were hungry and they plucked corn on the Sabbath. They, also, refer to the scriptures when JESUS healed on the Sabbath; the Pharisees complained that JESUS was working on the Sabbath.

EXPLANATION:
JESUS indicates his justification for the efforts on the Sabbath by two short statements.

1. In The Plucking Of Corn On The Sabbath—
    JESUS says—
    ("The sabbath was made for man, and not man for the sabbath.")
    JESUS does not want or require anyone to starve because it is the Sabbath. Refer to Mark Ch. 2, Vs. 23-28.

    Mark Ch. 2, Vs. 23-25&27
    "And it came to pass, that he went through the corn fields on the sabbath day: and his disciples

began, as they went, to pluck the ears of corn. And the Pharisees said unto him, Behold, why do they on the sabbath day that which is unlawful? And he said unto them, Have ye never read what David did, when he had need, and was a hungred, he, and they that were with him? How he went into the house of God in the days of Abiathar the high priest, and did eat showbread, which is not lawful to eat but for the priest, and gave also to them which were with him? And he said unto them, The sabbath was made for man, and not man for the sabbath.

2. In The Healing On The Sabbath—
JESUS Indicates—
(It is right to do good on the sabbath.)
During the work of God is always permitted, even on the Sabbath. Refer to Luke Ch. 13, Vs. 14,15&16.

<u>Luke Ch. 13, Vs. 14,15&16</u>
"And the ruler of the synagogue answer with indignation, because that Jesus had healed on the Sabbath day, and said unto the people, There are six days in which men ought to work: in them therefore come and be healed, and not sabbath day. The Lord then answered him, and said, Thou hypocrite, doth not each one of you on the sabbath loose his ox or his ass

from the stall, and lead him away to watering? And ought not this woman, being a daughter of Abraham, whom Satan hath bound, lo these eighteen years, be loosed from this bond on the sabbath day?"

If there is an emergency or critical need that happens the day of the Sabbath, JESUS does not expect you to ignore it. JESUS does not expect you to let someone   suffer or die because it is the Sabbath. This does not include other regularly scheduled jobs or occupations on the Sabbath to meet your family needs. Ministering is always permitted, even on the Sabbath. Except for the above, the work that is not permitted on the Sabbath is work that you do on the six other days of the week.

THE FOUR EASY STEPS TO GET SAVED/BORN AGAIN:

1. Repent:
   a. ask God to forgive your sins, ask in the name of Jesus;
   b. surrender your will for God's will to be done in your life.
2. Ask God to save you, to fill you with the Holy Ghost, ask in the name of Jesus.
3. Do not ask God anymore to save you, just thank God, praise God for saving you. You must thank God in the name of Jesus. At the

point of your greatest sincerity, you will speak in another language. This will be your sign of confirmation. God will be using your mouth to speak a language spoken somewhere on earth that you have not learned. This is your sign that you are born of the Spirit.

4.   Get baptized in the name of Jesus Christ.

<u>John Ch.3,Vs.3&5</u>
"Jesus answered...Except a man be born again, he cannot see the kingdom of God...Jesus answered... Except a man be born of water and of the Spirit he cannot enter into the kingdom of God."

<u>John Ch.3,V.8</u>
"...thou hearest the sound thereof...so is everyone that is born of the Spirit."

<u>Colossians Ch.3,V.17</u>
"And whatsoever ye do in word or deed, do all in the name of the Lord Jesus..."

CONTACT PAGE

We provide this page for those of you who desire to get in contact with us regarding:

I.   Ministering
   A. Preaching
   B. Singing
   C. Being prayed for
II. Ordering tapes
   A. Audio of this book
   B. Preaching
   C. Singing
   D. Additional end times prophecies
III. Ordering books
IV. Questions concerning our next book
V.   Other questions.

Remember to give your address. For a quicker response, provide a telephone number where you can be reached.

Frederick & Sylvia Franklin's
Ministry for JESUS
2669 Meadowview Drive
Mobile, AL, 36695
Telephone #: (251) 644-4329

ABOUT THE AUTHOR

"March Was When JESUS Was Born And Not Christmas" was written by Apostle Frederick E. Franklin of the ministry of F & SF Ministry For JESUS. What has been written is revelation from God that has been given to Frederick and his wife Sylvia. Frederick E. Franklin is an apostle, prophet and end times preacher. His wife, Sylvia Franklin, is a prophetess, evangelist and singer. The ministry positions stated above are what God, himself, has said/ordained and anointed them to be. Frederick and Sylvia have three children, Elijah Jeremiah Ezekiel Franklin, Daniel Isaiah Franklin, and Rebekah Anna Franklin. Frederick E. Franklin was a successful electrical engineer in private industry, state and federal government and also self-employment, before he was born again and told by God to preach.